ART & DESIGN

ACADEMY GROUP LTD
42 LEINSTER GARDENS, LONDON W2 3AN
TEL: 0171-402 2141 FAX: 0171-723 9540

EDITOR: Nicola Kearton
SUB EDITOR: Lucy Ryan
ART EDITOR: Andrea Bettella
CHIEF DESIGNER: Mario Bettella
DESIGNER: Sonia Brookes-Fisher

SUBSCRIPTION OFFICES:
UK: ACADEMY GROUP LTD
42 LEINSTER GARDENS
LONDON W2 3AN
TEL: 0171 402 2141 FAX: 0171723 9540

USA AND CANADA: VCH NEW YORK INC
SUITE 907, 220 EAST 23RD STREET
NEW YORK, NY 10010-4606, USA
TEL: (212) 683 8333 FAX: (212) 779 8890

ALL OTHER COUNTRIES:
VCH VERLAGSGESELLSCHAFT MBH
BOSCHSTRASSE 12, POSTFACH 101161
69451 WEINHEIM
FEDERAL REPUBLIC OF GERMANY
TEL: 06201 606 148 FAX: 06201 606 184

CONTENTS

ART & DESIGN **PROFILE** *No 48*

PAINTING IN THE AGE OF ARTIFICIAL INTELLIGENCE
Guest-edited by David Moos

Helmut Dorner, Untitled, 1994, oil and lacquer on plexiglass, 40 x 64cm

ANDREW BENJAMIN
WHAT IS ABSTRACTION?

'What is Abstraction?' Taking up Clement Greenberg's challenge 'We can only dispose of abstract art by assimilating it, by fighting our way through it' Andrew Benjamin addresses the question of abstraction, one of the most significant and influential developments in twentieth-century art and criticism. Picking key works such as Mondrian's *New York Boogie Woogie* and Jasper Johns' *Flag*, he argues that developments within abstraction have rendered the traditional theoretical and philosophical understandings inadequate. By looking at concepts of historical time and the notion of complexity, he develops a dynamic framework that allows for the reinterpretation and renewal of the tradition of abstraction. This is reinforced by a sustained encounter with contemporary abstract work by artists such as Lydia Dona, David Reed, Fabian Marcaccio, Helmut Dorner, Jonathan Lasker and Shirley Kaneda.

What is Abstraction? offers a thorough and incisive examination of the nature of abstraction which will undoubtedly enrich our understanding of twentieth-century art.

Other *What is . . . ?* titles include *What is Post-Modernism* (Fourth Edition), *What is Deconstruction?*, *What is Classicism?* and *What is Modernism?*

Paperback 1 85490 434 5
£8.95 DM26.00 $16.95
May 1996
68 pages
15 colour illustrations

*Further information can be obtained from
Academy Group Ltd, 42 Leinster Gardens, London W2
3AN, Tel: 0171 402 2141, Sales: 0171 402 3442
Fax: 0171 723 9540, or from your local sales office.*

*National Book Network, 4720 Boston Way, Lanham,
Maryland 20706, USA. Tel: (301) 459 3366
Fax: (301) 459 2118*

*VCH, Boschstrasse 12, Postfach 101161, 69451 Weinheim,
Federal Republic of Germany,
Tel: +49 6201 606 144 Fax: +49 6201 606 184*

HIDDEN CITIES, HIDDEN LONGINGS
NANCY WOLF
Karen A Franck

In the latest of our *Art & Design Monograph* series, American artist Nancy Wolf leads the reader through her life and her art, from her earliest work, when she first began commenting on architecture and society, to her most recent drawings, which pose compelling alternatives to the anonymous modern cityscape. Wolf vividly portrays the coldness and sterility of modernism, the superficiality of postmodernism, and the possibilities for change in deconstructivism. She has integrated her pointed critiques of these architectural movements with her own experiences – of alienation in a new urban renewal area in Washington, DC, of the urban devastation of New York in the 1970s and 80s, and of the warmth and intimacy of traditional communities in Africa and Asia.

Wolf's message is clear: contemporary Western architecture and planning have lost sight of people. Cities, buildings and public spaces leave inhabitants disconnected from each other and from the places where they live and work.

A foreword by Peter Blake, an introduction by Karen Franck and a lively, informal dialogue between Nancy and Karen frame the many spectacular images of Nancy's work. At times the tone is sombre but there is always a note of hope for a different kind of architecture – one that embraces people and celebrates community.

A retrospective exhibition of Nancy Wolf's work, 'Architecture Revealed', is to be shown at the American Institute of Architects in Washington, DC, in September 1996..

*Paperback 1 85490 351 9
£21.95 DM57.00 $38.00
July 1996
128 pages
141 illustrations*

the degree show

goldsmiths ba(hons) fine art and art history
exposed 28 june - 1 july   preview 27 june

goldsmiths college, university of london, new cross, se14 6nw tel. 0171 919 7171

PAINTING
IN THE AGE OF ARTIFICIAL INTELLIGENCE

Philip Taaffe, Rosette, *1987, mixed media on canvas, 304.8cm in diameter*

Art & Design

PAINTING
IN THE AGE OF ARTIFICIAL INTELLIGENCE

OPPOSITE: Fabian Marcaccio, Paint-Zone L.A. #1, *1995, 208.3 x 193 x 20.3cm; ABOVE, Moira Dryer,* Sister Sadie III, *1988, case in wood, 121.9 x 160cm*

ACADEMY EDITIONS • LONDON

Acknowledgements

We would like to thank all our contributors and especially our Guest-Editor David Moos for his time in putting together this issue of *Art & Design* on 'Painting in the Age of Artificial Intelligence'.

Unless otherwise stated, all images are courtesy of the artists: p1 Gagosian Gallery (New York); p2 Bravin Post Lee (New York); p3 Jay Gorney Modern Art (New York); **Introduction: Model Thought** *pp6-7* p6 Pace Wildenstein (New York); p7 Paula Cooper Gallery (New York); **Reinhardt Letter** *pp8-9* I would like to express my gratitude to Mrs Jane Lawrence Smith and Sarah Auld of the Tony Smith Estate for allowing me access to the material and for making available documents such as the Ad Reinhardt letter produced here (DM); **Sleep and Poetry** *pp10-13* Sperone Westwater (New York); **Cabbages, Raspberries and Video's Thin Brightness** *pp14-23* p17 (Centre) ACME (Santa Monica), and Tanya Bonakdar Gallery (New York), (Below) Galerie Max Hetzler (Cologne); p20 (Above) LA Louver (Venice, CA); **Il y a blanc de titre** *pp28-33* p28 (Above) Credac (Paris), (Below) Galérie E Manet (Paris); **Art and Art History in the New Museum** *pp34-39* text © Hans Belting; **The Shape of Meaning** *pp40-45* text © James Marrow, p41 Vienna Osterreichische Nationalbibliotek (Vienna), pp42-45 The British Library (London), photographs © Faksimile Verlag Luzern; **Matter's Insistence** *pp46-53* p47 Trustees of Dulwich Picture Gallery (London), pp48-50 Daniel Templon (Paris); **Architecture of the Mind** *pp54-63* p58 (Above) Galérie Philippe Casini (Paris), (Below) LA Louver (Venice, CA); p62 Pace Wildenstein (New York); **Foiled Again** *pp76-79* p76 (Above) Collection of the Art Gallery of Hamilton, Bruce Memorial, 1914, (Below) promised gift of Harry and Ann Malcolmson to the Art Gallery of Hamilton, p79 Alliance releasing; **Painting Theory Machines** *pp80-92* p81 Jay Gorney Modern Art (New York), p82 Barbara Gladstone Gallery (New York), p86 Rosemarie Schwarzwälder, Galerie Nächst St Stefan (Vienna)

Contributors' Biographies
David Moos is a curator and art historian who received his doctorate from Columbia University, New York. He is author, together with Rainer Crone, of *Kazimir Malevich: The Climax of Disclosure* and *Jonathan Lasker: Telling the Tales of Painting*. He is Visiting Professor at the University of Guelph, Canada. **Jonathan Lasker** is a painter who lives and works in New York. He regularly shows at the Sperone Westwater Gallery and will be having a travelling retrospective exhibition opening at the Kunsthalle in Bielefeld, Germany, early in 1997. **Jeremy Gilbert-Rolfe** is a painter who teaches in the MFA Program in the Fine Art Center, Pasadena, and is most recently the author of *Beyond Piety, Critical Essays on the Visual Arts, 1986-93*. **Jean-Luc Nancy** teaches at the Université des sciences humaines of Strasbourg where he is Director of the faculté de philosophie. His books include *L'absolu littéraire* (with Philippe Lacoue-Labarthe), *La communauté désoeuvrée*, *L'expérience de la liberté* and most recently, *Les Musées*. **Simon Sparks** is a graduate student in philosophy at the University of Warwick. He is editor of a forthcoming collection of papers by Jean-Luc Nancy and Philippe Lacoue-Labarthe and a collection of essays on Jean-Luc Nancy. **Stacey Spiegel** has been a fellow at the Center For Advanced Visual Study at the Massachusetts Institute of Technology and artist in residence at the Zentrum fur Kunst und Medientechnologie, Karlsruhe and the Banff Center, Canada. Recent exhibitions include Multimiela, Karlsruhe, Germany, Ars Electronica, Linz, Austria, Deaf95 Rotterdam, NL and Electra, Oslo, Norway. Spiegel is currently Adjunct Assistant Professor, Programme in Landscape Architecture at the University of Toronto; **James Marrow** is Professor of Art History at Princeton University, where he has taught since 1991. He has published widely on manuscript illumination and diverse aspects of late medieval religious art and iconography. **Hans Belting** has been Professor of Art History at Heidelberg, Munich, Columbia and Harvard. He is now Professor of Art History and Media Theory at the Hochschule für Gestaltung at Karlsruhe. His recent publications include *Likeness and Presence* and *The End of the History of Art?*; **Andrew Benjamin** is Senior Lecturer in the Department of Philosophy, University of Warwick. His publications include *Art, Mimesis and the Avant-Garde*, *The Plural Event* and *Object • Painting*. He is editor of the *Journal of Philosophy and the Visual Arts* published by Academy Editions, London; **Robert Yarber** was born in Dallas, Texas in 1948. He lives in New York City and Bellefonte, Pennsylvania. He currently teaches at Pennsylvania State University. Yarber is represented by Sonnabend Gallery in New York. He will be showing 'nocturnal landscape' paintings with the photography of Thomas Ruff at Sonnabend (New York) in May 96: **Ihor Holubizky** managed The Electric Gallery, Toronto in the late 1970s, dealing exclusively with art and technology. He held various curatorial positions at the Art Gallery at Harbourfront and The Power Plant, Toronto and since 1989 has worked at the Art Gallery of Hamilton, where he is currently Senior Curator; **Molly Nesbit** is a writer/teacher at Vassar College and contributing editor of *Artforum*. Her book, *Atget's Seven Albums* was published in 1993 by Yale University Press; **Darryl Turner** works with the intersection of images, sound and language in a variety of contexts. He has also done installation work with Hilton Als as well as artists pages and video projects in collaboration with Mr Als and Molly Nesbit, such as *Some Gesture Vehement and Lost* and *Continent/Incontinent* piece. **Warren Sack** is a media theorist, software designer and PhD student at the MIT Media Laboratory. His thesis work concerns the design and analysis of 'language machines' – software simulacra of reading and writing processes. Email: wsack@media.mit.ed URL: http://www.media.mit.edu/~wsack

FRONT COVER: Chuck Close, Lorna, (detail) 1995, oil on canvas, 259 x 213cm, (private collection), Pace Wildenstein (New York), photo Sarah Harper Gifford;
BACK COVER: Tony Scherman, Banquo's Funeral, 'Lady Macbeth', 1994, encaustic on canvas, 183 x 114cm, detail 1, Daniel Templon (Paris);
INSIDE FRONT COVER, Jonathan Lasker, The Divergence Of Truth And Beauty, 1994, oil on linen, 182.8 x 142.2cm, Sperone Westwater (New York);
INSIDE BACK COVER, Philip Taaffe, Mosaic, 1991, mixed media on linen, 284.8 x 189.2cm, Gagosian Gallery (New York)

EDITOR: Nicola Kearton SUB EDITOR: Lucy Ryan
ART EDITOR: Andrea Bettella CHIEF DESIGNER: Mario Bettella DESIGNER: Sonia Brooks-Fisher

First published in Great Britain in 1996 by *Art & Design* an imprint of
ACADEMY GROUP LTD, 42 LEINSTER GARDENS, LONDON W2 3AN
Member of the VCH Publishing Group
ISBN: 1 85490 232 6 (UK)

Distributed to the trade in the United States of America by
NATIONAL BOOK NETWORK, INC, 4720 BOSTON WAY, LANHAM, MARYLAND 20706

Printed and bound in Italy

Contents

Arrest of Christ, *British Library, London, Kings Ms 5, fol 12 (see pages 40-45)*
© *Faksimile Verlag Luzern*

ART & DESIGN PROFILE NO 48

PAINTING
IN THE AGE OF ARTIFICIAL INTELLIGENCE

Guest-edited by David Moos

INTRODUCTION
MODEL THOUGHT
David Moos

We want to float on the limits of consciousness – with mystery and knowledge. (Tony Smith, 1951[1])

In their final collaborative book *Qu'est-ce que la philosophie?* (1991), Gilles Deleuze the philosopher and Félix Guattari the psychoanalyst surmise the following criterion for the work of art:

> Percepts are no longer perceptions; they are independent of a state of those who experience them. Affects are no longer feelings or affections; they go beyond the strength of those who undergo them. Sensations, percepts, and affects are *beings* whose validity lies in themselves and exceeds any lived. They could be said to exist in the absence of man because man, as he is caught in stone, on the canvas, or by words, is himself a compound of percepts and affects. The work of art is a being of sensation and nothing else: it exists in itself.[2]

To cast the work of art as independent of man, as being able to exist 'in the absence of man', detaches painting from the realm of its creator and invests it with an ontology that may be autonomous. This visionary projection of the sensorial has proven a starting point around which to think of Painting in the Age of Artificial Intelligence. Concerning the constitution of man – as a collection of received sensorial and processed information of the world – the artwork is that which becomes man because it encompasses the human without being human.

Beyond this construct, which transfers subjectivity away from the creator/viewer investing it into the art object itself ('to extract a bloc of sensations, a pure being of sensations'[3]), one might also consider the method infusing realisation of this thought: namely, collaboration. At the close of this century Deleuze and Guattari together ineluctably confront the prospect that the Humanities are perhaps best marshalled through collaboration. The unitary mind sharply defines itself when operating at, or at least along the limits of cognition and imagination. Collaboration crosses the boundaries which inscribe received notions of subjectivity.

Collaboration knows no formulae except for a certain exchange of information. In this age of instantaneous communication, dialogue becomes possible in ways previously unimaginable. Culture has always been the great communicator, the bearer of human ideas. For art, as a keystone of culture, the interchange of information about individual contexts has often been the norm. What would be the relevance of discussing 'schools', 'movements', or 'trends', those cherished rubrics of art history, if one were not in search of how clusters of artists intersected to produce efflorescence at moments in the cultural imagination?

Ad Reinhardt, writing to his colleague Tony Smith[4] in 1954 (see pages 8-9), began with a summation of goings-on among vital members of what we now call The New York School. After an ironic listing of his colleagues' temperament, Reinhardt muses: 'that's all the news "out there", outside my studio, what I know of what the artists are up to is only what I call them'. What he 'calls them' is what is written in the letter, a statement that imbues writing with both the power of designation and constitution. Reinhardt suggests that one may fabricate the artists through writing, from the sequestered realm of the studio.

When James Marrow, writing in this issue, examines a Medieval 'Pauper's Bible' the dynamic power of words to condition images is presented at the root of the Western imagination. Marrow analyses how the artist and designer of *King's Ms 5* altered the way a manuscript conveyed meaning at the time, completely restructuring 'the user's understanding and experience of its contents.' Applying tri-coloured ink for the script, lavish hues for the images, and reformatting the organisation of the book as it existed until the early 15th century, the artist, Marrow notes, emblematically 'changed the protocols of reading and comprehending.' Such a sophisticated intertwining of image and text may adequately foreshadow the moment in which our multitextual, multimedia culture finds itself. With codes merging and boundaries blurring, the Medieval book as *unfolding* pictorial manifestation directly prefigures the computer-generated 'immersion environments' of an artist like Stacey Spiegel. Such trans-media constructs are eloquently reflected upon by Robert Yarber, a painter, who surmises that: 'if language speaks us, then pictures pose us, we are props in a grand *mise-en-scène*'. Here the word becomes both metaphor and herald of an image-based mind seeking intercourse with an essence residing beyond the world.

A glance at the concentration Reinhardt invests into his hand-writing clearly indicates the premium placed on the phrasing of thought, the *modelling* of thought onto the page. Reinhardt relies upon syntagmas, slides into a synthetic bi-linguistic blend of English and German, deploys diagrams, indices, lists, pressing the page to its thin limits. Such a letter, as historical document, informs the direction his painting assumed at the time while also anticipating the rigours demanded by future propositions. The private task of letter writing manifests an exegesis of self that describes the complexity of Reinhardt's intention with painting. With the attentiveness of a scribe, he forces the medium of writing to what Derrida, in a chapter entitled 'Meaning as Soliloquy', refers to as the irreality of inner discourse: 'Not only, then, does the imagination of the word, which is not the word imagined, not exist, but the *content* (the noema) of this imagination exists *even less* than the act'.[5] It is here that painting intervenes; that both

FROM LEFT TO RIGHT: Ad Reinhardt, Untitled, *1954, oil on canvas, 61 x 50.8cm; Tony Smith,* The Louisenberg #8, *1953-54, oil on canvas, 50.8 x 70.5cm*

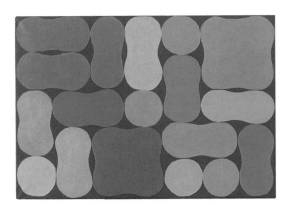

Reinhardt and Tony Smith turned to the canvas for reification of reality. For unlike the word, unlike the photographic image, the act of painting becomes paramount. In Jonathan Lasker's estimation: 'The painted world enjoys the sensuousness of being able to perceive the material world *through* matter.' It is *in* painting – where 'percepts are no longer perceptions' – that world and mind merge for moments of duration that become real, creating a narrative 'space of materiality', as Andrew Benjamin characterises paint's surface.

As talisman of the human, embodying a replete range of imagination's gesture, painting provides a horizon against which the artificial may design itself. If this is so, however, how can painting ensure its relevance in a future increasingly moulded by a technologically-driven consciousness? Will materiality prove painting's only recourse in the fast-moving environment of automated vision? Certainly, such romantic claims for the continuance of painting would whither tautologically; inevitably the culture would play itself out, becoming a parody of Formalist iterations.

The challenge rises from within technology itself. In 1970 Gene Youngblood, writing with a post-moon-walk McLuhan-inspired fervour, extolled expectation in technology's abiding quest for transparent communication:

> Just as the human nervous system is the analogue of the brain, television in symbiosis with the computer becomes the analogue of the total brain of world man . . . It allows us to see ourselves and, through fiber optics, to see inside ourselves. The videosphere transcends telepathy.[6]

The utopian desire for unmediated, interconnected 'telepathy' is an old dream – old as the Middle Ages, reiterated in the era of telecommunication. Unlike technological conduits, in painting the structure and fabric of intelligence is incarnated. Painting is more than a functional component of the world-brain; it is rather the content-giving device from which intelligence acquires specificity. Painting, according to Jeremy Gilbert-Rolfe, manages to subsume technology's immanence:

> The screen is hard, the image ephemeral, substance subsumed into transmission. The video image provides no way through which the image may return to the world; because of this, the fascination for the sense in which video is everything painting is not, is held.

Stranded out there, ceaselessly circulating but never fixed, the 'videosphere' (Youngblood) is proliferation void of place, profile lacking location. Video, says Gilbert-Rolfe, 'offers painting another surface to which to refer', and in this sense merely becomes fluid collaborator in painting's involvement with the world.

Involvement, however, is not synonymous with any object *per se*. Painting is buoyed through its ability to both absorb and respond; it is the being to which the world returns and in this sense it will never be permitted passage into the world as such. Jean-Luc Nancy inscribes the transpiring of painting as instigating a certain 'taking' – a seizing, usurping, or grasping that grapples with both 'beginning-and-end', both the 'saying' and the 'thing':

> For what there is there, is nothing; not anything that could take place either in the time-space of the world, nor outside of it as if in an other world beyond this one. What there is, there is the '*il y a*', the 'there is', the taking-place itself . . .

The transactional capacity of painting frames an otherness to which the world may seek belonging.

Perpetuality ushers discourse towards 'Painting Theory Machines' where, computer scientist Warren Sack enables the painted image to produce flows akin to those Deleuzean agglomerations which allow for other connections to be made. Such a topology, as typology, evades the machine's grid, is unfigurable without painting. In terms of software engineering, Sack adduces, the mingled frisson of intellect and intuition that painting provokes comes to delineate a machine that would be impossible to build. Yet that, of course, becomes the fuel of painting theory machines.

Such detailed consideration, occurring in the precise, magnified space where disciplines abrade, posits definitions of the Artificial at the nexus of transpiring Intelligence. The essays presented in this issue of *Art & Design*, constituting 'sensation' verbally, depict the life-worlds of conversation with artworks. In the being of human communication, which may be a way of periodising the present, articulation tumbles to its future. Outside subjectivity the painting lives, it thrives, in the precipice that divides the chromatic surface of video's 'thin brightness' from the integument of mind that the media of painting becomes. The be-coming of the transactional mind, its structure as articulation; this will be the task of painting in an age of artificial reason.

Notes

1 Tony Smith, *Pointy Hat in S. O. [South Orange, NJ],* c1951, unpublished manuscript, Tony Smith Estate, New York.

2 Gilles Deleuze and Félix Guattari, *What Is Philosophy?,* Columbia University Press, New York, 1994, p164.

3 *ibid,* p167.

4 Smith lived in Germany from 1953 to 1955.

5 Jacques Derrida, *Speech and Phenomena and Other Essays on Husserl's Theory of Signs,* Northwestern University Press, Evanston, IL, 1973, p47.

6 Gene Youngblood, *Expanded Cinema,* EP Dutton & Co., New York , 1970, p260.

DEAR TONY: I'VE ALERTED SOME ARTISTS BY QUICK POSTAL-CARD, SINCE I'M NOT TALKING TO ANY OF THEM, OF THE NEW GERMAN SCHOOL OF PAINTING LED BY ANTON SCHMIDT KNOWN AS THE POST-NEW-YORK-SCHOOL, THE FIRST MOVEMENT OF THE SECOND-HALF OF THE TWENTIETH CENTURY AND A NOT BAD CAREER WITH SOME POSSIBILITIES, PERHAPS, OF FAME, FORTUNE, EVEN MONEY, MAYBE, IF ONE CAN SELL ONESELF, ONE'S WORK, TEACH, AND GET A PRINCE-BISHOP. AS AUGUST COMES TO A CLOSE, BETTY'S IN MEXICO, MARK'S GOT THE GOUT, THE EIGHTH STREET MOVEMENT'S STILL OUT IN EASTHAMPTON, STILL IS WRITING ME POISON-PEN-NOTE FOR WHICH HE GOT A FOUL-WORDED-POST-CARD IN RETURN, MOTHERWELL'S STILL MAD AT ME FOR AN ARTICLE WHICH I WROTE CALLING HIM AN EDUCATIONAL-SHOP-KEEPER, A TRAVELING-DESIGN-SALESMAN, AN ART-DIGEST-PHILOSOPHER-POET, AND A PROFESSORIAL-BUTTON-HOLER, CAN YOU IMAGINE ANYBODY GETTING SORE JUST FOR THAT? I ALSO CALLED HIM A COOK'S-TOUR-GUIDE-&INTERPRETER THROUGH MODERN ART.   SINCE THAT'S ALL THE NEWS "OUT THERE", OUTSIDE MY STUDIO, WHAT I KNOW OF WHAT THE ARTISTS ARE UP TO IS ONLY WHAT I CALL THEM.   SO THEN, ABOUT MYSELF, MAYBE I'LL TRY, IN THE NEXT DECADE, TO BE-COME "THE PROTESTANT PAINTER" SINCE SUCH EMINENT THEOLOGIANS AS PAUL TILLICH HAS LIKED MY WORK AND HAS TRIED TO MAKE THE AESTHETIC EXPERIENCE ITSELF, A RELIGIOUS PROBLEM, AND NOT LIKE THOSE ROMAN-CATHOLIC-DECORATORS LIKE MATISSE, LEGER, OR THOSE GREEK-ORTHODOX-PROPAGANDISTS LIKE PICASSO, OR THOSE JEWS, ALL OVER THE PLACE, LIKE CHAGALL, BLOOM, KOOTZ, GOODMAN, GOTTLIEB, MOTHERWELL AND FERBER. IF YOU CAN, SEE "NEWSWEEK", PAGE 53, AUGUST 23, 1954 "PIETY IN PAINT" OR "#12 NON-OBJECTIVE-MYSTICISM?"   SO, AS FAR AS I CAN SEE, WITH MY INNER-EYE, YOU HAVE ONLY THE NEO-RELIGIOUS-AVANT-GARDISTS TO WORRY ABOUT, AS COMPETITION, INCLUDING ME, OF COURSE, FOR I'M NOT GOING TO STAND BY AND SEE SOME SÜDDEUTSCHER MUSCLE IN ON ALL THE GIMMICKS AND GRAVY, WHICH IS HARDLY ENOUGH TO GO AROUND AS IT IS, IT BEING ALL ONE CAN DO TO KEEP BODY AND SOUL TOGETHER THESE DAYS, WITHOUT YOU BECOMING A PARTNER IN OUR BUSINESSES, I'LL SAY.   THE ONLY OTHER THING THAT MIGHT INTEREST YOU WAS MY GETTING AN INVITATION TO MAKE A SUGGESTION, ALONG WITH HARRISON, DREYFUS, ROBSJOHN-GIBBINGS, STEINBERG, SINCE THE METROPOLITAN MUSEUM HAS REDECORATED ITS INSIDE, FOR THE REDESIGNING OF ITS EXTERIOR, A SORT OF GAG FOR THE HERALD-TRIBUNE'S-MAGAZINE-ON-SUNDAYS.   EVERYONE TURNED IT DOWN BECAUSE OF ARCHITETHICS (COMBOWORD) OR BEING TOO BUSY. BUT I OFFERED TO DO THEM ALL SO I MADE THESE SUGGESTIONS (THEY'RE TO BE PICTURES, RETOUCHED PHOTOS, ETC) (1) THE MET AS "ARTMOBILE" A FASHIONABLE IDEA IN THE SUBURBS AND WEST NOW, THE "MUSEUM ON WHEELS", (2) THE MET AS "IMAGINARY MUSEUM" AS MALRAUX'S "MUS-EUM" "WITHOUT WALLS" (3) THE MET AS 100% "AMERICAN" REDESIGNED IN THE "STICK" STYLE OR ANY "GRASS-ROOTS-MID-WESTERN-FRAME-HOUSE-MANNER" (4) THE MET AS "STORE", X-MAS CARDS, JEWELRY, BOOKS, PEPSI-COLA, POSTAGE-STAMP-REPRODUCTIONS, ETC. AND (5) (6) (7) (8) (9) THE MET AS REDESIGNED ACCORDING TO ITS ATTITUDES AND POLICIES ON ART, HISTORY, CULTURE, AS A POPULAR AND PUBLIC INSTITUTION WITH AN ATTENDANCE LARGER ANNUALLY THAN THE YANKEE STADIUM, ETC..   BUT THE GUY TURNED IT DOWN AND I REALIZED I REALLY DIDN'T WANT TO DO THE THING ANYWAY, BECAUSE I'M NOT MAD AT THE MET AND I WOULDN'T DO IT JUST ONLY FOR THE GAG, BECAUSE I WANT TO BE LIKE MEYER SHAPIRO AND SHOUT AT FRANCIS HENRY TAYLOR FOR SOME GOOD REASON, HEY?   BUT, AS YOU CAN SEE, THERE ARE ARCHITECTURAL OPPOR-TUNITIES COMING THROUGH AND YOU JUST BECOME ANTON SCHMIDT AND IT'LL BE RIGHT

QUICK AS A FLASH, FRANK LLOYD REINHARDT OF MCKIM, MEAD & KOOTZ.　　　YOU KNOW I TOOK SEVERAL SHOTS OF THAT JAPANESE PRINT I SENT YOU BECAUSE IT WAS ALL OVER PARIS AND VERY PARISIAN AND WOULD HAVE SEEMED SHOCKING TO SEE IN AS MANY PLACES IN ANY OTHER BIG CITY, BESIDE IT RELATING TO JANE & CHILD, RITA & CHILD, AND MADONNAS & CHILDRENS EVERWEAR.　　　I READ A BOOK YESTERDAY BY HERMAN HESSE IN WHICH A GIRL TEACHES A WEREWOLF TYPE OF GUY TO DO THE FOX TROT! HO, HO!　　　YOU KNOW, I'M HAVING TROUBLE READING THOSE PLANS YOU SENT, I KNOW DOORS AND MAYBE STAIRS WHEN I SEE THEM THAT WAY BUT I'M NOT SURE OF CIRCLES AND CROSSES AND SOME SQUARES, ESPECIALLY WHEN THEY'RE NOT IN COLOR. WHAT'S WRONG WITH MAKING THIS TYPE OF HONEST-TO-GOODNESS-DRAWING, ENCLOSED (A) DESIGN NO. 4?　　　I LIKE CHURCH PLANS, GRUND-NISSEN? SO WIE (B)(D)(C), FIG.S 97, 9, & 8, ENCLOSED.　　　LATELY I'VE BEEN THINKING ABOUT THE CRUCIFORM, THE CROSS & PLUS SIGN, THE T, E WITHOUT THE MIDDLE LINE, L (THE ANCIENT CHINESE MIRROR T,V,L DESIGN WITHOUT THE V), THE SQUARE ⊔, POST & LINTEL ∏? PIE SIGN? THE CHINESE SIGN FOR "ABOVE" 丄 AND "EARTH" 土
⊓ "BORDER", ⊔ "RECEPTACLE", "BOX" ⊏ "MOUTH" ☐ & "ENCLOSURE", "SAY" & "SUN" 日, "TEN" 十, "ONE" 一, "MAN" |, "FIELD" & "LAND" 田, "MIDDLE" 中 AND "WORK" 工, "OLD" 古 & "EARLY" 早, "RETURN" & "TIME 回, & "SELF" 己, ETC.

　　　FOUR DIRECTIONS, ABOVE & BELOW, CROSS-ROADS, TREE, CROSS, RIGHT-LEFT, VERTICAL "FIGURE", HORIZONTAL "LANDSCAPE", ETC., CAN YOU ADD ANYTHING TO THESE 4 ELEMENTS, 4 SEASONS, 4 BEASTS, 4 EVANGELISTS, GUNSIGHT-FRAME-BEAM? OR DO YOU KNOW ONLY ABOUT STARS AND HOOPS?

　　　I'M GLAD YOU'RE FEELING LESS STRAIN, AS YOU SAY IN YOUR LETTER, ABER BITTE ENTSCHULDIGEN SIE NICHT SOFORT ALSO BITTE ENTSCHULDIGEN SIE MICH FÜR SCHREIBEN SO VIEL ABER ICH BIN IM STUDIO UND SEHR MÜDE UND FELT LIKE WRITING ALL THIS, HABEN MICH HART GEARBEITET UND FÜR LANGE ZEIT MICH IN MEIN SELBST ODER SICH GECONTEMPLATED MEINE BELLY BUTTON UND WERDE EXHAUSTED UND SO GEHE ICH NACH DEM JACKDANIELSSOURMASHSCHNAPS DAS IST VIEL BESSER THAN DEINE ITALIENISCHER ROTWEIN.

　　　DIE NEWMANS ODER BB'S, ANSWERING NICHT DER TELEPHONE SO MÜSSEN SIE VIELEICHT AWAY GEGANGEN HABEN ETWAS EIN BISCHEN VACATION ZU ENJOYING ALSO ANALEE MUST SOON ZÜRICK ZU ARBEIT GEHEN NACH LABORDAY, SO WIR EXPECTING ZU HÖREN VON ZEM ZOON.

　　　UND DAS IST ALLES WAS ICH HABE ZU DU ZU SAGEN JETZT, MAYBE IN EIN PAAR WOCHE, DIE KÜNSTLER COMIN ZÜRICK TO THE CITY, UND VIELEICHT HABEN SIE ETWAS NEUS ODER GESCHICHTE ZU REPORTING...

　　　ABER WIR SIND FEELING GUT, RITACHEN, ANNACHEN, UND AD GLÜCKLICHES WÜNSCHEN NACH DEINE TWEI HÜBSCHEN MÄDCHEN UND DEINSELF SCHREIBE MEHR WENN ZU ZEIT HAST!

The Consciousness of Animals, *1994, oil on linen, 190.5 x 190.5cm*

SLEEP AND POETRY
THE CONSCIOUSNESS OF ANIMALS
Jonathan Lasker

One of the pleasures of reading literature written centuries ago is that it illuminates forms of perception and viewpoints which may since have become atrophied. I felt this was particularly true when I recently read John Keats' *Sleep and Poetry*. In that poem, Keats expressed his belief in the power of dreams, either in sleep or in verse, to transcend mortal reality by conjuring the realm of the divine, and thus to illuminate the spiritual universality of our consciousness.

The early 19th century was a time when one could still express such faith. By the 20th, the imaginative capacities of the human mind had become psychoanalysed, turned into mechanical processes that express only existential human needs. In our age, human consciousness is losing ground in both the arena of epistemological certainty and the realm of spiritual transcendence which, in a universe of objective mechanical causes, is no longer believed to exist. Its once exalted status is being further eroded as we enter the age of artificial intelligence.

As a painter, I feel that the human mind as confronted by artificial intelligence may be compared to the medium of painting as it was confronted by the invention of the camera. Much as the camera appeared capable of objectively rendering an image better than painting could, the computer appears capable of objectively knowing our world better than we can.

In both cases the power of humans to depict their world, either by hand or through conception, has been devalued, or at least relegated to the less valued realm of imaginative as opposed to objective rendering.

It has been asserted that there is a lie in all mimesis. If this is so, it is as true for a photograph of a hillside as it is for a painting of a hillside. It is also true for computer programs no matter how sophisticated they may be. In each case, neither a thing (a camera, a computer) nor an animal can know another thing other than through its own inherent epistemological capabilities: mechanical processes for things and subjective perceptions for animals. In this sense, a camera or a computer is no less a subject in relation to another object than is a human being.

If mimesis is a lie, there is, furthermore, a lie in the existence of the camera and computer as they exist only to create a mimesis of a scene or a mimetic explication of the physical properties of an object. They do not exist naturally. They do not exist for themselves. Human perceptions may be founded on lies, but in our being we *know* the truth of our existence. *We are*: the image of a thing *is not*. Since our consciousness is participatory in our being, its ontological purpose is assured. This we can take to be real.

Our perceptions of truth are thus often skewed to reflect the ultimate reality of our existence in nature, in the cosmic order of things. By our nature, when we perceive we seek a truth that is more than literal. There may be an untruth in any representation of a landscape, but in a painting there is the truth of natural materiality. The painted world enjoys the sensuousness of being able to perceive the material world *through* matter. Painting, unlike the bodiless images of photography, never leaves the natural world of things. The sunflowers of Van Gogh are at once a depiction of nature and nature itself – the physicality of existing materials like ochre and burnt sienna. Painting always refers back to its own constituent materials. As such, it is as close as culture ever gets to nature.

Mechanical perception – artificial intelligence – can never do more than understand things in their particularity. This is a function of its wholly literal epistemology. It is not equipped to understand things universally. Such an understanding (fundamental as it may be) is essentially imaginative. It is through the imagination that we can contemplate the possibility of a bigger reality. For this reason, it is important for us to maintain a connection to a vision independent of mechanical prosthesis; a vision which is purely animal. Our rationalistic obsession with objective intelligence is overvalued.

Perhaps it is time to enhance our appreciation of those qualities of consciousness which we share with other natural beings, the qualities of imagination and sublimation which we bring to our perception of the universe and which stem from our affection for the condition of being. This affection seems oddly inexplicable if being is viewed as stemming from purely material or mechanical causes.

It may be time for a rudimentary faith of the sort Keats expressed in *Sleep and Poetry*, a faith that being and consciousness have purpose and meaning. A faith in the transcendent capabilities of the human imagination, with its epistemological and its ontological understanding of reality.

Perhaps our universe is as some American Indians thought it; that our life here is a dream and when we die we go elsewhere to dream. If so, what reality could we conjure with the dreams that come to us in our sleep, and in our art?

Let Us Become Ultimate, *1994, oil on linen, 190 x 254cm*

Supplemental Reality, *1995, oil on linen, 152.4 x 203.2cm*

CABBAGES, RASPBERRIES, AND VIDEO'S THIN BRIGHTNESS

Jeremy Gilbert-Rolfe

To go by the poetic experience and the most ancient tradition of thinking, the word gives Being. Our thinking, then, would have to seek the word, the giver which itself is never given, in this 'there is that which gives' . . . The whole spook about the 'givenness' of things, which many people justly fear, is blown away. But what is memorable remains, indeed it only now comes to radiant light.[1]

Intuition is unfashionable at the moment, but it seems relevant here. Kant altered the role of intuition by giving it a priority which made it at once judgmental and at the same time the condition for a further judgement. Where Descartes, Locke, and Leibnitz had shuffled it around in various ways that permitted it to be the link between sense impressions and reason, Kant made intuition occur coincidentally with – or both before and after – sense impressions, so that one's impression of the world was also an intuition of a degree of pleasure or pain; a judgement about whether one liked it. From there, thinking could become a judgement of one's judgement which reexamined the intuition discursively, confirming it or modifying it as the case may be. No-one, I think, has any doubt that it is through such a process that paintings get made – of course, that itself has been used to argue that paintings should in fact no longer be made at all – but it raises a question about artificial intelligence. Presumably, artificial intelligence is pure in its intellectuality in that it needs no sense of pleasure or pain to guide it. It responds instantaneously to sense data which are, for it, already and exclusively discursive. I have suggested elsewhere that the purely, or exclusively, discursive is where we find the sublime nowadays, and that, for us, the sublime is a techno-sublime.[2] I am concerned here with some relationships which might be seen to exist between painting and the products of that history of technology which has the possibility of an artificial intelligence as its implicit goal.

I am interested in how things look and what that implies. It seems clear to me that where painting has in the past been comparable to other media and objects, its relationship to the video screen alters the terms of such a comparison. I arrived at this thought in the following way: I was thinking of Martin Heidegger, all of whose worst dreams have come true in terms which are quite consistent with his own, and of the question of intensity as a characteristic of phenomena. I shall say here that the video image is one of intensification – it makes the world more than it is, more colourful, more defined – which at the same time robs things of their substance. Heidegger would not have liked it very much, I think it is safe to say, for that reason among others.

Which brings me to cabbages and raspberries, the one tough, the other delicate, and both surely familiar to Heidegger. Heidegger talks about strawberries growing on a hill in the passage from which the above quote is extracted – wild ones, presumably, as opposed to the kind that grow in greenhouses or at least with plenty of straw and attention to keep the frost off – but I prefer to recall raspberries – which also grow wild on hillsides – because their form contains the principle of liquidity.

A cabbage can be deep green and is itself fleshy, substantial, replete with structure as form, delicate at its extremities and firm at its core. A raspberry, on a grey day – on a hill, say – is a very intense spot of colour. As a thing it is very fragile, light; its taste as intense as its colour. A painting could, in Heidegger's terms, treat either as an essay in substance and essence, or the recognition of the one as a return to the other. It would be in the substantiality of painting that the essence of the object would be reconvened as manipulated substance. This would not be true, it seems to me, of the video image. The screen is hard, the image ephemeral, substance subsumed into transmission. It is in substituting transmission for substance – as opposed to painting's use of one substance to interpret another – that video announces, or institutes, its identity as an other, as belonging to a world of meaning (communicated intent) whose terms derive from, and lead, elsewhere than painting's can, and Heidegger thought they should. This is the sense in which video is everything that painting is not and in which it therefore holds such a fascination for it: in so far as its origin in electronic transmission gives it a purely technological identity, it provides no way in which its images may return to the world of manipulated substance (a point demonstrated by visible manipulation of the video image always meaning that video is at that moment being made to behave like a painting).

What it offers painting is another surface to which to refer, in this case, one which is brighter than any that preceded it, unimaginably thin – describable only as an exterior when viewed

Gabrielle Jennings, still from To Whom It May Concern, *1994, 30 minute video,*

as an object, a surface without depth – and continuous by definition. Everything that painting is not: an uninterrupted surface born of pure reason. What (provided one is not Heidegger) could be more seductive?

This is the sense in which I want to think of the history of technology as the history of surfaces and colours. If technology's history is one of the extension of human capacities towards the posthuman – conquering physical space, not to mention the people who have the (mis)fortune to live in it, that sort of thing, with the retrospectively implicit goal of achieving a condition in which people are in theory if not practice ultimately to become redundant – Lyotard's brain in a space capsule, surviving the end of the universe; Baudrillard's capitalist machine run by little white rats once it has found a solution to the need for human consumers – then it is in that constantly inventing artificial bodies, originally produced as simulations of those that already exist. The surface and colour to which video appeals, in which it lives, is plastic.

Barthes compared plastic, the culminatory techno-surface, to skin in that both are continuous, which is to say that objects made out of that material simulate the condition of the body in its original, pre-technological, condition. There had been a plastic surface before, the surface of painting, but that had been a plasticity made out of openings, interruption, and conjuncture. A plasticity of morsellation, made out of adding up and layering and even reconsidering. Plastic's most obvious point of comparison to painting is its status as the first continuous surface which, in not being an accumulation or combination – not built or woven or otherwise assembled – is a thing, rather than an image, with the properties of the photograph. One adds to that the evenness and clarity of plastic, properties generally found desirable in flesh, and it may be possible to say that it is in plastic that one first sees the emergence of the brightness associated above with video.

Plastic began by simulating wood, early bakelite, the dashboards of cars in the 40s and 50s, but soon took over the world with its own colours, the pastel shades of the 60s, the lipstick and shoe colours of the more recent past. Plastic objects generally have to be shiny, hence shoes and lip gloss as referents: think about what picking up a shiny black telephone and speaking into it most obviously resembles. The length of the head and that of the foot are the same, one's hand is as long as one's face, telephones are, like shoes, detachable adjuncts, telephones are coloured like shoes not like hands or faces – or feet. Indeed, Gabrielle Jennings tells me that the television show *Get Smart*, made in the 60s during plastic's brief Heroic phase, featured a telephone shaped like a shoe.

Plastic, unlike oil paint, comes in two conditions: things which are touched and held, like telephones and keyboards, and that which – like paintings – exists only to be seen, the screen. In this sense video is continuous with a world of objects whereas paint is not. The arrival of plastic's brightness was slightly ahead of that of colour video – also pastel during the 60s, now similarly capable of greater intensity. Both replace the brightness of the world with a greater brightness, and in both cases this is a brightness which is primarily understood as technological. That is to say, while one's admiration of the way in which a medieval (European or Islamic) miniature also replaces the world with a greater brightness may begin with an appreciation of the qualities of gouache and coloured ink, it is likely to lead to a theologico-philosophical appreciation of what that greater brightness is (supposed to be) about, whereas plastic or video propose themselves as conditions in which the technological level is not transcended, leads nowhere, but is already theological-philosophical. Moreover, rather than propose another condition, it subsumes within itself those with which it might be compared. Where in a medieval illumination figures might be larger or smaller in accordance with their possession of divine grace, and brighter than those in the real world by virtue of the elimination of shadows in the interest of a theologically-derived requirement for completeness, the colour of the telephone is familiar but only from within the world of plastic; the video image replaces its referent by being more like it than the thing itself.

If one may say that no one looks as good in real life as she does on the screen, then one may at the same time note that in the Middle Ages a comparable sentiment could have meant something quite different. Furthermore, while they may be compared with other objects those made out of plastic are, as often as not, things that did not exist at all before plastic itself, such as telephones, or computers, or electric coffee grinders. As objects, their pre-plastic history is antecedent, lost in that of the objects they replaced: the note delivered by a servant who would wait for a reply (or the cryptic and ambiguous telegram); the elaborate Victorian contraption using punch cards; the simple mechanical device fetishised by Duchamp, artist of symbolist nostalgia.

John Gage has pointed out that 19th-century naturalism, emerging from that of the preceding half-century, amounted to a significant change in painting in that it required the repression of identifiable properties of the medium and facture in the pursuit of a reconvention of the experience of nature.[3] It was now important that paint seem to take on the characteristics of what it represented in a way, or with a thoroughness, that it previously had not. The effect of this unprecedented and fundamental thoroughness was to lead painting's materiality towards the immaterial: this kind of representation was to be founded not in convincingly representing materials, lace or flesh or silk or fur – as was, for example, the desire for mimesis of earlier painters in Venice or Holland – but in depicting atmospheres, climactic conditions, states of vibrancy or decay. The modern call for a 'truth to materials' is, then, reactive. Before naturalism, there was never an artificiality so great as to replace the truth of the material. Gage describes the history of colour usage in the West and begins with theories which relate the palette to the colours iron turns when it is being heated up, so that black is at one end and white at the other with red in the middle, and with attitudes to colour's application which forbade mixing colours and instead relied on cross-hatching, so that mixed colours were seen as combinations of essences rather than as degradations of essences (called, in philosophy, as once were all combinations and derivatives of essences, 'accidents'). Theologico-philosophical from the start, such approaches never knew anything but a preoccupation with the truth of materials. Just before the arrival of naturalism – roughly contemporaneous, as we now realise, with the beginning of nature's disappearance into its own preservation, culminating in it now comprising that which the state has preserved in a park – there was a fashion for paintings with cracked varnish called 'crackle'. Again, the possibility of at least playing with a kind of truth; the look of the historical; the poetics, as it were, of an image historicised in its content and also its constitution (of a past activated by and preserved in an image which contains an idea of its pastness). What was played with was the truth of materials. When it reemerged, it was a secular and de-historicised truth, the thick light of Impressionism.

Because if Gage is right about naturalism requiring that the medium disappear in favour of what it depicts, one may say that John Constable and others ushered in a change in the notion of the world and what mediates it. My concern here is with seeing naturalism as the origin of the antecedents of colour video, which I propose as the light of a plastic world. The antecedents I have in mind are Impressionist painting and

colour photography, and in that both seem to frustrate the kind of reading which Heidegger performs in *The Origin of the Work of Art*, they may be seen as intermediate stages between naturalism's identification of its medium with sensation in the presence of nature, and video's electronic intensification of data as sensation. Taking a Greek temple as an example, Heidegger draws conclusions from the fact that it is made out of the rock on which it stands. The temple itself is at once Temple and substance, World and Earth, the transformational passage between the two, the capacity of the one to maintain that of which it is a transformation, is what Heidegger thinks one is looking at.[4]

To experience the work is to experience the gap between the two as the realisation of the essence of the one by the other where the act of realising is also what keeps them apart. Certainly one could look at many paintings in such a way. Medieval miniatures come to mind once again, made as these were out of art materials whose origins were known and recognisable while directed towards an essentialism. Or Vermeer, constantly adjusting painting technique to the material to be represented, so that the painting is an elaborate identification of perception with method – the thingness of the thing calling forth a particular deployment of paint.[5] But that's not, one gathers, how one is meant to look at John Constable, and it seems impossible to do with the Impressionists in the sense that the materials they worked with have an origin deep within the bowels not only of the earth but of technology. Earth colours, the colours of crushed sea animals, and the metallic colours which are the basis of painting's brilliance, were supplemented for the Impressionists by industrial colours, of no recognisable origin in either the natural world or the age of iron (an age which, in its simplicity, might have been technologically acceptable to Heidegger).

The Impressionists, doctrinally committed to reconstituting the brightness of daylight, were obliged to the inventiveness of the German petro-chemical industry, which gave them alizarin crimson, viridian, and other colours necessary to the task of simulating the natural which are in themselves unnatural in every obvious sense except that they do indeed exist in nature. Or do they? Consider this. One painter paints a red butterfly in the 18th century, a second paints another at the end of the 19th. A connoisseur, Heideggerian in bent, looks at both. In the one, the colours mixed to make the butterfly's red lead off towards minerals manipulated by elementary physics and crushed shell fish; in the other towards the Ruhr and industrial chemistry. In the latter case, the butterfly's red is no longer seen by a perception developed in response to simple technology, but to a more complex one in which material origin is, as a matter of course, inconceivable except as a formula facilitated by a machine. The origins of perception are less clearly in the earth as a visible earth, perception as recognition (as Heidegger wants it to be) has nothing to recognise. In these terms it can only recognise – Heidegger's nightmare – an ungrounded ground, colours which are truthful but have no recognisable origin as matter. One could relate this to Galileo's having to prove Aristotle wrong. Aristotle insisted that what is visible to the naked eye is superior as information to that gained through the use of an instrument, Galileo had to prove that the telescope was right and the eye wrong, that the moon may look smooth but in fact is cratered. Impressionism is the art of a culture that has long since conceded that a truth comes from the instrument that need no longer be confirmed by the senses themselves. The material origin of colour as paint played no part in the choices an Impressionist painter made, the passage from what a colour is to what it can do in approximating a perceptual condition was complete.

There is a further sense in which I want to propose Impressionism as an antecedent for video colour that underscores this. Patti Podesta has pointed out to me that one cannot have muddy colour in video. There's no black in Impressionism and no mud in video. Where everyone from Plato to Goethe had wanted to see colour as an accidental consequence of black and white, the Impressionists sought the reverse. The shoes about which Heidegger was so passionate would never have been returned to the blackness of the signified if they had been painted by Monet rather than Van Gogh (there's a lot of other things they would not have been either) but would instead of found themselves deoriginated in the light which fell upon them, in all that they were not: white infinitely subdivided. By the same token, from wherever video looks at the world and the earth it has largely replaced it finds an origin for the image in a schematised division of white light. Like the colours of medieval painting, video has no need of the impure. Unlike medieval painting and because of its foundation in a naturalist aesthetic, video has plenty of pictures of mud and the muddy: like Impressionism, it presents that which cannot be found in its own constituents.

I offer the following precession, which depends for its formulation on Gage's account of naturalism as the tendency which precluded truth to materials. One could do it either with Heidegger's temple or with the painting he makes up out of several Van Goghs which he seems to have confused with one another. The precession is from a grounded sign, a sign concerned to recall its origin and to signify through that recollection, to a sign grounded in its own ungroundedness: from Heidegger's work of art, through Impressionism, and thence to video colour.

Consider three things: Heidegger's temple, Monet's paintings of Rouen Cathedral, any video image of an old building made out of stone. The temple is made out of the materials on which it stands, enabling it to be both stone and an image made out of stone which takes the properties of stone – pre-technological but containing the essence of the threat of technology. The Monet, on the other hand, is a thick painting in which the air,

FROM ABOVE: Christian Haub, Soft, 1994, acrylic on paper and acrylite, 76.2 x 76.2 x 1.9cm; Uta Barth, Field #8, 58.4 x 73 x 5.1cm, 1995, colour photograph mounted on panel; Stephen Prina, Galerie Max Hetzler, Installation Galerie Max Hetzler, 1991, toned gelatin silver print, 12.7 x 10.2cm (frame size, 30 x 27.6cm)

17

the sky above and the atmosphere all around, robs the stone facade of its pre-eminent materiality: it is no more or less substantial than all that it is not including emptiness and insubstantiality itself. And the video image? It has no weight at all. The building and the screen are joined by light. Neither is present to the other through thickness of any kind, but are continuous with one another through a light which shines from within. Video realises the ambition of Impressionism in that it replaces substance with light in a way unavailable to painting. Not only can it not be muddy it is also not a kind of mud. It does not share a ground, cannot return to it, with its referent. It has, perhaps one could say, no recognisable relationship to the essences it seeks to recall. Neither as a material object which signifies, in its own materiality, a continuity with that to which it refers – unlike the temple, and also unlike Monet, where painting dematerialises the cathedral through an emphatic materiality of its own – nor through visible transformation, which is to say, through duration made visible.

The Heideggerian nightmare is two-fold here. All things have become equally insubstantial, mediated by a medium which has no correlation with things as substances – it is not stone transformed, it is not a process in the sense that painting is visibly that, a passage with an end which has concealed but reflects its beginning – and it is also instantaneous and automatic. It is materially discontinuous, as a fabricated object or sign, with the world whose image it presents (or produces), and it makes time invisible. Things cannot exist without time but in video, unlike temple construction or Impressionist painting, time is photographic: technological time, duration conceived as an instant; duration, therefore, as invisible to the naked eye as is the origin of alizarin crimson.

Colour photography, unlike paintings and temples, is seamless like the body and the plastic object and a consequence of the same industrial technology which gave the Impressionists alizarin. Like vision, or the mind's idea of vision, it is presented all at once to the camera as an impression, and emerges all at once – as a simultaneity rather than an accumulation – in the developing fluid. The video image, adding movement which is not an accumulation of frames but once again seamless, takes the photographic to a logical conclusion, but first a word about the colour photograph, which has an emulsified surface so thin that you cannot see it as a thing, and a paper support which is inseparable from it. Painting's fascination with photography has always taken two directions: towards the photographic's capacity for clarity; and towards its ability to record the opposite, dispersal, vaporousness, atmosphere.

Uta Barth's photographs suggest painting in the sense that they could remind one of Gerhard Richter's fuzzy photo paintings, which is to say, of paintings of photographs. In this they demonstrate that the nagging challenge that photography offers painting is not about verisimilitude, but continuity. What does a Richter do? Of course it does a lot of other things too, but it also reminds one of the impossibility of simultaneity in painting, particularly when it addresses the instantaneous. The heterogeneity of painting's surface forecloses access for it to the continuum of the instant which comes naturally to the homogenous surface of the photograph. A surface, moreover, which is unlike painting in that – as Barth's photograph shows – for one part to be in focus is for another not to be. Nothing of the sort is true for painting, whose heterogeneity guarantees that it will be a mass of foci all uncomfortably related to each other.

One further point about photography. In suggesting that the contemporary object aspires to the condition of plastic even when it is of necessity made of something else, I would also suggest that normative colour is nowadays photographic colour, and that nowhere is this more true than in the area of tonality (colourlessness). The grey test card, the pure condition of colour photography, surely provides a zero condition for colour comparable to the zero condition for the object offered by plastic's extruded or moulded continuity. (It is also relevant here that the equivalent in video is 'white balance'.) As a zero condition of another kind, a hand-toned contact print of a grey card stood in for a Richter in a project undertaken by Stephen Prina at the Max Hetzler Gallery in Cologne in 1991.[6] Prina documented every show the gallery had held since its inception, substituting an alternately horizontally and vertically oriented photograph of a grey card for every exhibition for which the gallery did not have an installation shot. Richter's 1982 show of lavish abstract paintings was therefore represented by a vertical rectangle reminiscent of the monochrome paintings of a few years earlier. Richter's career is founded on relationships between painting and the look of the photographic, and it seems poetic, if not ironic, that a grey card that stands in for one of his paintings ends up referring to one he actually made. I also see it as a return to the question I just raised about grey.

I have suggested that photo grey is a zero degree for us. In an essay to which I have already referred, I point out that a photo-test coloured backdrop is the pure context of the fashion photograph, the place where the model as sign is ultimately free to be that: a sign for and of the fashionable. (Also that Richter's paintings exist to end as photographs in art magazines.) The point I want to make is that for photo grey to have achieved that status, photography would have had to displace painting as a normative referent, which it has. It is photo grey we recognise (in painting there's always a choice of two, it is binary, like the computer) not Davies Grey or Paynes Grey.[7] I suggest it is the same for colour itself. Painting, especially non-representational painting, can nowadays only refer to the colours of plastic/colour photography/video (all the same thing), either affirmatively or by ignoring them: their presence is implicit. They have replaced the colours of the natural with a now naturalised intensity.

This question returns one to cabbages and raspberries, while also suggesting that for non-representational painting at

FROM ABOVE: Nancy Haynes, Molly's Soliloquy, *1991, oil on linen, 24 x 34cm; Fandra Chang,* Untitled, *1996, ink on canvas, anodised aluminium and plastics, 14.9 x 14.9 x 1.3cm*

least, Heidegger's nightmare may be Deleuze's quite nice day.

Indeed, already in Maupassant, naturalism is nothing but a facade: things are seen as if through a window-pane or on the stage of a theatre, preventing duration from forming a coarse substance in the process of degradation; and when the pane thaws, it gives way to running water, which cannot be further reconciled with originary worlds, their impulses, their fragments and their outlines.[8]

Like cabbages and raspberries, paintings are things. They may or may not be images, in the sense of having a referent – a landscape or a fuzzy interior – but as things that are meant to be seen they function as images. As such, they invite comparison with the images which surround them, and it is in these terms if no others that I want to compare the work of four artists with the surface of video, a plastic surface brighter than daylight. It would be silly to discuss the large paintings of Pollock and Newman without some reference to the space of cinema – of, actually, Cinemascope – and it is in similar terms that I am invoking video's hard but continuous surface in regard to the paintings of Nancy Haynes, Fandra Chang, Christian Haub, and Fabian Marcaccio.

At first sight Haynes' paintings seem to be indifferent to the recognisably technological, but when one takes into account that she makes paintings which glow in the dark, other points of comparison begin to emerge. Chang works with the accumulative and discontinuous, but I am struck by the kind of layering and accident that is characteristic of her work and by it being a function of the juxtaposition of screens. Haub brings painting to bear on a hard and light-filled plastic surface – Plexiglass – working with a convergence between the endless referentiality and mutability of the one and the blank implacability of the other. Marcaccio's *Paint-Zone L.A. #5*, (1995), suggests to me a screen-like identity for painting, reminiscent of the space created by video even while it is not of or about video.

Nancy Haynes' work is directly comparable to Chang's in two respects: the technique or method is protracted and slow and involved with layering and not immune to chance, and the result, in both cases, is a surface which proposes an image or idea about flow or movement rather than form or structure. One could also make a direct comparison between Haynes' murkiness and Haub's blurredness, in that in both, colour and surface are similarly atmospheric. Here, however, I am more concerned with a general question about how one sees a 'Haynes'. I've already said that one could see it as ignoring the video screen (and the colour photograph and the plastic surface which precede it), but that would be to say that the work was lost in negation. I think it is more appropriate to suggest that one sees a Haynes painting as protracted instantaneity, a surface organised less around incident than around formlessness.

In so far as they propose formlessness, they simultaneously propose an indeterminate depth. Haynes' paintings are characteristically matte, but to me, their atmospheric spatiality suggests a relationship between what her work does and the experience of looking at television. Video cannot ever be matte; it is bright and shiny, like a varnished painting where depth is in part achieved by glazing. Glazing means colour suspended in varnish, pigment magnified by oxidised and clarified oil, glowing from within like a television. In so far as depth is a function of glazing, it is one of fluidity, fluidity being therefore capable of both depth and the possibility of a surface which is not tied to an image of a skeleton or armature. Glazing proposes or presents a density, the matte surface an expansiveness which less obviously places a surface between the viewer and what the viewer is looking at: one looks through or into glazes, but at matte surfaces. In modern religious shorthand, matte means the honest object, glazing the tricky illusion – the given space of authenticity invaded by a depth which is not its own, an objection analogous at some level to the Church protesting that single-point perspective amounted to the invasion of God's space by a secular point of view, in both cases the invasion of that which is by a force which is not of it, and in both the substitution, as it happens, of uncertainty for the certain. But Haynes' matteness is not a form of shorthand, but an elaborate and protracted rediscovery of a pictorial depth made out of layering and erasure – neither available to video – presented as neither but rather as a continuum. Which is the point here. Everything in the painting is a return to painting as it always (and therefore never) was, except for the space it contains. The space it contains is the space that non-representational painting makes when video has offered it the possibility of space as one movement rather than a meeting of movements.

Hayne's paintings are matte, either black or grey or a colour that video could not reproduce. They possess a space which can be returned to the history of painting without reference to video if one so desires, but glow from within and take place entirely on a surface which is uninterrupted as is that of the video screen: not a negation in any sense, but surely an equivalent. As such, Haynes' paintings suspend the space of nature – atmosphere – somewhere in a world of activity and materials, which may or may not lead back to a body – a gesturing, living body, or a corpus of painting history, as one prefers – but which also may be read as painting becoming video, a movement of intensities knowable only as that, which is to say, as not so much disembodied as never having been a body.

Disembodiment as a process which intensifies what was never embodied is what one gets from Chang. Chang uses a laborious method to arrive at the work as an assembly of separate components, in which ink is first rolled onto a coarse screen (so that the ink stays in some areas and falls through elsewhere) which is then photographed to produce both positive and negative images of the screen. The work is then made out of both the original screen and its positive and negative images. Multiplicitous – involving multiplication through the recombination of derivatives which, in being combined, deoriginate that from which they derive – these works play with simultaneity in a manner comparable to the effect created by erasure and addition in Haynes. What leads one to video here, however, is an idea less of flow than of intensities, which is to say of transmission rather than embodiment. If the model for pictorial order was once the abstract idea of quantitative expressions of the possession of grace, and subsequently that of a mind that converted sense data into reason (the Enlightenment mind preserved in the possibility of artificial intelligence), and after that to a sensibility which knew itself through reconsideration (addition, and erasure as addition), then that to which Chang's pictorial order appeals would have to be the video screen, although once again as an equivalent rather than a negation, and once again maintaining that equivalence through doing what video cannot do – by preserving material differences where video begins with their elimination. As an array of intensities, Chang's works reembody nothing so much as they present something which is not a body. In this, Chang's works return one to the statement of Heidegger's with which I began this essay. If it is the word that gives things their identity as such ('gives Being'), and if one may locate the word's own being only through its deferral into what it facilitates (ie, as 'the giver which itself is never given'), while it is only in the word that things find themselves – the thingness of things – then painting has to be recognised as a thing which is also a practice (ie, never entirely a thing) before any painting-as-thing can make painting-as-word (ie, as a concept contained in a practice) gives anything; which is to say, before anything will happen *in* it.

What is given with Chang is painting ungrounded, painting as both discontinuity and its opposite, hyper-continuity, before and after and now joined inextricably as event.[9] In Chang's most recent works, she begins with a small stretcher, from the art store, which she then paints one colour. Then she rolls ink onto it through a screen, which makes an impression which reveals the stretcher. She takes the stretcher to a lab and has it photographed in a negative and positive image. One of these images is then printed on a sheet of Plexiglass (what the English call Perspex) which is then placed over a piece of metal or paper on which either the negative or positive image – sometimes the same as the one on the Plexiglas, other times not – has also been printed. By the time the process is complete, black dots which had begun by referring to the raised bits of the canvas' weave have come to look like digital dots, and the soft and interrupted surface of canvas has been replaced by hard and unbroken plastic. What is on the surface of the plastic points to an interior which has no more to do with where the work began than it does to what one is actually looking at and simultaneously – a mutual deferral – to what is not there.

A passage from a very enjoyable book which discusses

video in terms of Heidegger and Deleuze underlines the kind of equivalence for it that I find in Chang:

> With video, the mechanical movements that break up the instantaneous and charge up the continuous are in fact inseparable . . . What some descriptions of television register as fragmentation, reification, and formal hetero-geneity can be more fully grasped as diffracted slices of still time, and what strikes us as television's compression of distance and presence is perhaps best understood as its capacity for automatic time.'[10]

With Chang one would only, but significantly, need a definition of the mechanical which included the intuitive and of the automatic that could encompass the accidental.

Which brings me to my last two painters and also to my conclusion. Heidegger's nightmare is Deleuze's quite nice day because where for Martin the human gets lost in technological extension (its intensification as function) which leads away from itself, for Gilles you can always add something else on. With Deleuze, the mind as transmitter and receiver always finds not itself but a self, the one it needs at the moment, in the outside that meets its own outside. Furthermore, what it attaches itself to, finds itself through or within or in convergence with, is a principle received (perceived, recognised) as a type of force. Little Hans sees that a cart horse has more in common with an ox than a race horse, and as such thinks of being as action and in action rather than in identity as genealogy. Projection and reception replace the question of origin; returning will literally get you nowhere. I am told that many in the field have thrown up their hands at the idea of artificial intelligence because it is remorselessly pre-Kantian, which is expressed as an inability on the part of computers to manage pattern-recognition, and prefer instead to talk about 'intelligence enhancement'. The intelligence is human and the computer is added on.[11]

Haub's *Soft*, (1994) adds paint and paper to a Plexiglass surface. Painting meets the implacable and steals light from it, the interrupted and accumulated coloured surface both supported and ungrounded by its support, which takes in and gives out light and can be seen to do so. Intensification takes place not on the surface but in the support, behind the surface, before the painting. I was reminded recently that for Shakespeare 'before' meant 'in front of' in the sense of 'yet to occur'. The physically internal light of *Soft* supports the painting's surface while being modified by it, lies behind that surface (which leads straight to it) while reflecting and deflecting light and the image of the surface onto the wall around the painting's perimeter. At the same time the support is one thing (like light) where the painting involves many actions and reconsiderations. Transparent, which paint can never be, where the painting is atmospheric. Continuous, a surface joined to its other side, interior inseparable from exterior, where paint is a surface always in need of a support, and each speck of paint separable into pigment and oil. Two kinds of movement: movement of interruption and

degree, which is painting as human movement, movement from the translucent to the opaque, movement as pausing and reconsidering (going forward by returning); and the uninterrupted and constant movement of light, movement as continuity and sameness, which is plastic as technological movement, imperceptible speed and intensification (a state of convergence from which return is inconceivable).

I end with Marcaccio because he does effect a kind of return and one which brings one back to a point made here in relation to photography, which is that paintings cannot be out of focus. The atmospheric in Haynes or Haub is a blurring of that which was never not a blur, which is never true of a photograph – but is of the video signal, unless you are an artificial intelligence. Painting's artificiality permits it to be about focus and therefore never to be that or to be never anything but. As such it must always construct a subjectivity (not actually clearly singular because of being) spread out over a surface rather than surrounded by a space: starting and restarting here and also here and here, rather than being there.

Video colour is tied to a thinness effect. It takes place on and in a surface one looks at. Its origins are in oil painting because that – as glazing – is the measure of colourfulness. It is depth as intensity, rather than substance, and in its continuity it plays another game of equivalence with oil painting as a glazed surface by way of the look of homogeneity derived from its photographic identity. Marcaccio's *Paint-Zone L.A. #5* could be seen to play with that idea of thin and continuous depth. It remembers painting without putting its members back together, in the isolated and recurrent *trompe l'oeil* images of woven canvas that recall the surface the painting replaces, causing the work as a whole to be an irregular alternation of references to canvas and passages of white, connected by a meandering line. What takes place on the surface of this painting is, perhaps, only describable as surface rather than depth, but as such it is a surface detached from what it points towards – back towards the woven support it has replaced and in that retained, and forwards towards a whiteness within or across which meandering can take place. Whiteness stands for: the (invisible) combination of all the colours in light; the place of inscription as line; absence (of inscription-expression-visible activity): blankness; and extension as both flatness and depth.

When naturalism's facade turns to running water, according to Deleuze, flow replaces the outline and the fragment, situating all in an unsituated movement of de-origination.[12] But flow is still understandable by humans as animals, one can be caught up in it and even imagine resisting it. Beneath and behind it lies electricity, endless and imperceptible impulse, holding everything together and holding everything apart. This is understandable only by humans as intelligences, as a fact outside and within the body but inaccessible to it – and also as the way video works. Once white was the white of the page; Manet-Mallarmé's pages pregnant with meaning; and then of the wall – Ryman, undifferentiated white framing white as differentiation. But now, perhaps painting – which always found itself somewhere else as the world found itself in painting – finds white leading it towards that which it cannot be: the principle of the same as a function of the imperceptible; force without material substantiality; the thin and brilliant light of video.

And what does painting learn from video (and from plastic and from colour photography)? If from whiteness as pregnant meaning it learnt how to survive the fall of naturalism through the potential of the object, and from white as the undifferentiated the terms of whiteness as interruption and therefore differentiation

through attaching it to a substance (paint) which was continuous with a practice (painting), from video it learns the secret of the electronic, that there are no gaps, that presence and deferral are indistinguishable in a sheet of clear Plexiglass, that there is movement in interruption. Like Impressionism, video is never still. In that inability to be still while always being shallow and brighter than the world painting finds itself – which is what it found in the page and the wall – always and as ever an artificial intelligence focused on a blur, the meeting point being the surface and the depth it must both imply and fail to be.

Notes

1 Martin Heidegger, *On the Way to Language*, 'The Nature of Language', Peter D Hertz (trans), Harper, San Francisco, 1971, p88.

2 Jeremy Gilbert-Rolfe, *Das Schone und das Erhabene in der Gegenwart*, 5, 'Das Erscheinen des post-human im Erharbenen der Technologie', aus dem Englischen von Dagmar Demming/Almuth Carstens, Merve Verlag, Berlin, forthcoming 1996.

3 John Gage, *Colour and Culture, Practice and Meaning from Antiquity to Abstraction*, Boston, Little, Brown & Co, 1993, pp105-11. *See also* Chapters 9 and 11.

4 As Eugene Kaelin puts it: 'In so far as these two dimensions – the earth and the world – become related in experience, neither takes precedence over the other, since the work is perceived to be working to the degree that a functional relationship is established between the earthly dimension (nature) and the worldly (the culture). Eradicate the one or the other of these dimensions, and the work disappears; change the one or the other, and the work's tension is changed.' *See* EF Kaelin, *On Texts and Textuality: A Philosophy of Literature as Fine Art*, Rodopi, Amsterdam, forthcoming 1996.

5 *See* Norman Bryson, *Word and Image, French Painting of the Ancien Regime*, Cambridge University Press, Cambridge, 1981, pp24-25.

6 The artist has described the work as follows: 'In the case of the Richter photo, as is the case for all of the photographs of photographic grey cards, a 4 x 5in, black and white negative was shot directly from the grey card. All of the photographs in the project were contact printed directly on to photographic fibre paper, with the frame margin exposed and printed. They were then sepia-toned by hand. The photographs have ivory-coloured mattes and frames of walnut-stained mahogany', fax to the author, Dec 29th, 1995.

7 As also: lemon or cadmium yellow, cerulean or ultramarine blue, viridian or emerald green, scarlet or crimson.

8 Gilles Deleuze, *Cinema 1. The Movement Image*, Hugh Tomlinson and Barbara Habberjam (trans), University of Minnesota Press, Minneapolis, 1986, p133.

9 There may be another sense in which Chang's painting is ungrounded, which has nothing to do with the subject at hand. There is the question of Chang's relationship to the Euro-American painting tradition. The question of Asian art as having more to do with passages between than with essences as cores or interiors could well be raised in regard to what she does to that tradition. Needless to say one will get nowhere by just lumping Chang into some category, in the implicitly distasteful way in which Terry Myers links her to the Vietnamese film maker Trinh Min Ha in the catalogue to the recent Corcoran Bienal, which is about as much use as lumping Matisse together with Dziga Vertov on the grounds that they are both European. A serious investigation of her – and others' – works as multicultural in the kind of deorigination they produce would, however, be exciting.

10 Richard Dienst, *Still Life in Real Time, Theory after Television*, Durham, Duke University Press, North Carolina, 1994, p160.

11 I am indebted for this information to my colleague Peter Lunenfeld, of the graduate faculty in the Program in Communication and New Media Design, Art Center, Pasadena.

12 I have addressed the importance of Deleuze's notion of flow to non-representational painting elsewhere. *See* Jeremy Gilbert-Rolfe, *Beyond Piety, Critical Essays in the Visual Arts 1986-1993*, Cambridge University Press, New York, 1995, p51 and *passim*.

EMERGING SPACE
FROM PLATO'S CAVE TO THE ROTTERDAM HARBOUR SIMULATOR
Stacey Spiegel

What we need is a language which shall copy nature
(Bertrand Russell)

We are teetering on the brink of the next millennium, awash in a culture of transformation and riding a wave of utopian innovation that promises to reconfigure the very means of communication. It is here amongst the thousands of news groups and web-masters, providers and users that we find ourselves peering through the immaterial – into cyberspace. There, flowing through the ether of the networks is the poetic intersection of media (technology) and content (perceptual experience) that in purely psychological terms is an 'aesthetic experience' – the weaving of information with sensation as a means for reorientation and relocation of self. Here, in contrast to the avaricious search for the dynamic that has become a potent metaphor of our culture, we can move beyond travel logs and terrestrial territory, in search of the gravitational pull of new sublime landscapes.

In a world of changing paradigms, it is easy to get lost in the swirling discourse that defines information technology as an aesthetic, perceptual and cognitive vehicle. Listening (as if one could sustain the blare of the jargon) to the language of data communication specialists, one realises the evolutionary lineage of computational modelling is suffering from a rather narrow and uninspired perspective in the area of visual and aesthetic expression. Discussions about virtuality have not only denied a historical context, but simply have become aesthetic by addressing the technological flow of information without reference to either experience or consciousness.

On the whole, the activity of constructing meaningful perception and reconnecting individuals with a sense of location and orientation has been fundamental to artistic practice. Yet somehow, even within the art and design community, there are those who are hesitant to embark on the intellectual/emotional investigation of new domains in cyberspace. Their defence is woven from the fabric of the arts and crafts tradition and they resist the desire to form meaning from the immateriality of virtual information space. Curiously, this position may in fact be a most reactionary choice as we trace the lineage of immersion spaces from a historical perspective.

Microbiological research in the area of human cells suggests that the encoded evolutionary history of the gene lay dormant in each molecule. In transposing this methodology to observing today's state of electronic expression we can trace an evolutionary path that extends from early Gothic cathedrals to Omnimax and beyond. Functionally aesthetic, immersion spaces constitute a culturally relevant form for electronic media, and in a genetic model that bares this lineage, each historical movement lies dormant and encoded. It is significant in looking at immersion environments that we recognise these references and their impact and influence in the visceral development of cyberspace.

In the context of the desire for a merging of content and information the artistic potential of a truly hybrid experiential virtual environment called 'immersion space' has evolved – multi-perceptual, interactive three-dimensional navigational form of spatial experience, 'morphed' from the collision of visualisation's history and the current ability for real-time computational modelling. One way to think about this is that virtual immersion spaces are to cyberspace what electricity is to energy. As is the case with most of our current visualisation technology, real-time immersion environments are an outgrowth of military technology: technology focused on the transcription of nature into a machine language that simulated the real world as an experience of virtuality. In other words, the early graphic capabilities for machines to 'see' and 'recognise' the human world quickly evolved into machines that generated perceptually convincing representational models for humans to explore a virtual world.

The mechanisation of nature into a transcribable and mechanical format has become a predictable indicator of reality for the simulator environment. Popularised in the American movie *Apollo 13* is the image of astronauts stranded in space only to be rescued at the last moment by flicking the right sequence of switches, which was figured out in Houston's earthbound simulator. Today, exploring interactive extra-terrestrial experience here on earth is both the training ground of pilots and thrill seekers alike, depending on which NASA tour you are taking. Once the suspension of disbelief is achieved, the responding human interfaces with the computational accuracy of the machine, accounting for the sophisticated real-time training now given to infantrymen, airline pilots and sea captains. With the increased horsepower of networked graphics computers, simulators have the potential to be much more; immersion spaces are the front line in the exploration of interactive and sensory approximation of virtuality, making tangible the intersection between self and machine.

Intuitively, one rejects the hyped Virtual Reality head-mounted gear or goggles with the wacky glasses that stick TV monitors in your eyes. These are primary tools of distortion and disembodiment, isolating the viewer from a shared discourse and removed from human contact. Rather, the immersion environment is a real physical space that supports the simultaneous participation of a public – a finely tuned system of networked computers generating a navigational three-dimensional model, coupled to projectors that create a seamless panorama of 360 degrees, linked to a digitally activated hydraulic motion platform and, of course, digital sound.

Crossings is an artwork that, on the invitation of DEAF 95, stretched its own boundaries and definitions to explore the potential of the world's largest marine immersion environment – the Rotterdam Harbour Simulator of Marine Safety International, Rotterdam, Holland, in November 1995. This simulator, located in the concrete core of a structure designed by architect Norman Foster, is a silo 25 metres in diameter. The image plane runs 360 degrees around the room and is the full height of the outer wall. One enters from below grade and arrives in the centre of the room in front of a hydraulic motion platform. The steel cabin mounted on the platform is designed like the bridge of a North Sea ferry; on top of it sit 12 synchronised high-resolution image projectors, projecting the full computer generated image 30 times a second to create the seamless 360 degree full-colour panorama. The complex nature of the environment necessitated substantial modification on site to the software tool set called Polytrim which was brought from the Centre for Landscape Research at the University of Toronto. The upgrade in technology was to facilitate the ability through software to generate a dynamic immersive landscape with full motion and sound. Woven into this landscape were information structures that supported links to the information space of the World Wide Web.

This theoretical terrain was ten by five kilometres in size and had congealed areas of content that one could identify in space as one wandered about. These sites were referred to as Oasis, Dead Space, Data Fields and Info Community. Each space is a compositional element whose shape and character is derived from the encoded content. Within the context of the larger landscape, the sites are proportionately scaled and dynamically reflect the varied sensory information layered within. The act of decoding the landscape layers is a contemporary alternative to the hierarchical and dualistic constraints imposed in earlier times. The transparent infrastructure of the technology supports the powerful sensation of one floating, immersed in perceptual space. A deeply compelling and emotionally charged sensation through the interaction with information structures characterises the aesthetic core of a contemporary metaculture.

Crossings is based on the metaphoric power of landscape as a non-hierarchical dynamic space. It asserts that art is not merely transcriptive in the sense of conveying information, but is also a transformative process which results in the construction and reconstruction of reality as an aesthetic experience. To that extent, the traditional distinction between reality and virtuality disappears when one is in an immersive environment. The artificial dualism of information and sensation is eliminated and the interactive unfolding of a personal narrative occurs in a sensual environment where live links to the World Wide Web occupy the formal pictorial space. By accepting *Crossings* as an evolutionary step that extends painting beyond cinema, one might argue the genealogical family of aesthetic investigations begins in the deep regions of the Palaeolithic cave.

Possibly the first example of immersion space begins in the metaphoric and philosophical Platoian cave or the visually dynamic caves in the region of Les Trois Frères in Arièges, France. A more interesting discussion might come out of observing how preliterate societies rapidly evolved immersion spaces such as the 5th-century Baptistery of the Orthodox in Ravenna. Here, one finds an example where the mosaic montaging of Christian and Islamic narratives encodes the entire architectural volume. The interweaving of image and structure became a dynamic and impressionistic force when fused with ritual practice. Knowledge and social practice were grounded in the aesthetic and the surrounding narrative scenes became virtual spaces for personal habitation.

The evolution of the cathedral, and of the cupola in particular, demonstrates the reoccurring use of immersion space as created through painterly treatment of spatial form. Few are as compelling as the frescoes that fill the Cathedral of Parma by Correggio, the recognised precursor of Baroque painting where immersive environments were formalised as the primary educational technology of the time.

Modern art institutions have replaced these immersive spaces of the cathedrals and attempted to reduce the quantitative experience through formal sensory limitations. Today one wanders the corridors and galleries of international museums searching for pictorial immersion which can be found in a qualified state in the paintings of Morris Louis, who opted for sensation through the painterly diffusion of light. In a genetic link to empower painting once again – possibly reflecting on the passion that has been lost for the spectacle of the panorama – institutions like the Museum of Modern Art in New York have installed the Impressionist panoramas of Monet's *Water Lilies* to a semi-immersive condition.

In the public domain, the desire for immersive spaces as non-formal aesthetic devices were popularised by Robert Baker who, in 1792, developed a painterly device called the Panorama. Not unlike the Imax of today, entire buildings were created to house the enormous stretched canvas. Running the entire inside of the rotunda, the full-scale painted image slowly rotated around seated spectators. In semi-darkness, the audience gazed at the continuously moving image lit by candle from above. By 1845, new technologies precipitated the invention of the Phantasmagoria. This device often presented in a church environment combined multiple magic lanterns that were controlled to project moving apparitions onto ground glass sheets that completely surrounded the audience.

Not long after, the Dioramas, invented by Daguerre, replaced the Panorama. Once again, the gigantic paintings were exhibited in specially designed buildings. Here, the interior space revolved around the image and the spectators peered out through windows that moved across the surface of the image. These paintings, however, were on a transparent medium and their dynamic force was expressed through constantly changing light. In the same period, photographic techniques allowed for the assembling of negatives to create long seamless panoramas which quickly found their way into film and animations. One only has to consider the use of the sublime landscape as a device in early narrative film to recognise the immersive power that provided orientation and location to the narrative. The intensity of involvement with the sublime was the source of experimental 360 degree cinema in the Bell pavilion at Canada's Expo '67 in Montréal. Imax, born from the invention of panorama film, surrounded the spectator with a representational environment whose narrative moved through time. The compelling power of the immersive image convinced the eye that it was in fact the spectator moving through space.

Crafted through technology, Imax and Omnimax – like their predecessors the Panorama and Diorama – can be shown in specially designed architectural structures. The passive spectacle of a monumental experience of sensation is the potency of Imax's technology. Documenting the wonders of nature, the image presence, however, cannot shift scale or resolution, and is left to fulfil the avaricious desire for eccentric travel logs. Contemporary image technologies suggest that imbedded into representational images are encoded many layers of information, and the limitation in understanding these is constrained by one's ability to interact with the information. The late Doc Eggerton from MIT, famous for the invention of strobiographic photography – images of stop-motion, such as the bullet caught as it passes through a card – would in a lecture hold up a photographic satellite image. He described film as a storage medium and images as encoded information. 'You have to know how to read an image,' he would say and proceed to describe what he saw in that generic photographic image; everything from geographical location to geological character to celestial time to local temperature, humidity, wind and so on, as he moved to finer and finer grain detail.

The decoding of information in layered and encoded terrain has been the foundation of scientific practice. In recent years, medical imaging has facilitated a virtual portrait of a patient's pathology. But once you set functional use of the image aside, what aesthetic structures are encoded in this pictorial space?

In *Crossings*, the sublime in landscape is presented as an interactive and immersive pictorial space that extends pictorial lineage beyond cinema. Ideologically, it is a metaphoric terrain in cyberspace, a three-dimensional model whose encoded structure dynamically responds to the layering of information; a macro-environment through which the wandering viewer personally deconstructs the spatial convergence of information and content into aesthetic experience.

Immersion environments manifest through electronic media are an evolutionary component of our cultural identity. They transform our multidimensional world into a comprehensible and meaningful place, as Giotto accomplished in Padua. Immersive environments are the required vehicle to wander into the pictorial depths of immateriality. Cyberspace, currently seen as an undefined terrain, is freed from the shackles of formal artistic practice. Yet in exploring the aesthetic potential for communication, we return to Russell's thoughts on nature. In his day, they may have been characteristic, however, the implications for our cultural identity rest in our ability to develop a transformative rather than a transcriptive language in order to interpret Nature.

IL Y A BLANC DE TITRE[1]

Jean-Luc Nancy

Il y a blanc de titre et c'est peut-être ainsi que ça commence.

There is white of title and it is perhaps in this way that it begins. What? One cannot say it. One cannot say at the beginning *what* begins. One cannot even say at the beginning that it begins. When one says it, when one says '*ça commence*', it has already begun, and consequently already finished beginning: it begins to finish. One cannot say where it begins, nor when – which amounts to the same: one and the same space – time which one cannot express [*dire*].[2]

But this does not quite mean that one would have to keep it quiet, nor that the white blank of title would correspond to a religious paralysis at the entrance of a shrine. It does not mean that one would have to reserve and preserve the secret of this beginning and of this ending of beginning – of this ending which begins in the beginning long before the beginning itself begins, of this ending which begins the beginning, which breaches its opening [*ouverture*]. It does not mean that there would be a mysterious silence there, one which would have to be contemplated in silence.

For what there is there, is nothing; not anything that could take place either in the time-space of the world, nor outside of it as if in an other world beyond this one. What there is, there is the '*il y a*', the 'there is', the taking-place itself; this is not some thing but rather, the beginning-and-end of some thing. This is '*Il y a*', 'There is', itself and in person, which amounts to saying: neither any one nor any thing, but the thing itself, such that in itself the appearing [*le paraître*][3] drowns it – and the thing consents[4] to this.

One cannot say it, because there is nothing to say: nothing at all [*rien du tout*], nothing of a totality which would be one of substance and form, of surface and foundation, of beginning and end; and nothing consequently to be said regarding any part of a whole which has absented itself in presence. One cannot even say that one cannot say it. Anyone who might happen to say, here and now, that one cannot say it – this person would have had to have already come from elsewhere and have already said or heard said, elsewhere, what one can and cannot say. He would have to have the knowledge of this world and of an other world, of this meaning [*sens*] and of an other meaning, of this saying [*ce dire*] and of an other saying, one which would consist of keeping silent.

Here and now no-one has yet come. It [*Ça*] simply comes, and it begins. Precisely, it just finishes coming from elsewhere and preceding itself in a past. This past is itself past (it has as much ceased to finish as it has ceased to begin), which is to say, nothing has happened – and one cannot even say that nothing has 'yet' happened, because there is no space-time for such a 'still not yet'. There has been no watching, no waiting, nor preparation, nor formation, nor promise, nor anguish. And precisely this too: that there *was* nothing, is nothing necessarily about which to remain silent, since there is nothing there which could be said or about which one could be silent. There is no 'there', no 'over there', caught, lost, absent. There is no absence. Or rather: it is absence itself in presence. It is for this reason that one cannot say 'one cannot say it'. There is neither the impossibility of speaking, nor the obligation of silence. Which means there is neither aphasia, nor ecstasy, nor inhumanity, nor religion. There is: *that it begins* – this alone, very exactly: the beginning-here-and-now without elsewhere, neither past nor future. This through which there is a 'here-and-now'. There is silencing it, and thus there is no longer the need to say it as if, before my intention to speak, there was something there, set down like an inert, formless or obscure thing which would await one's coming to seize it and mould it into signification. There is no hidden meaning [*sens*], nor a machine built in order to express it. The meaning [*le sens*] which is there, is disposed wholly otherwise: like something obvious, like the obviousness of something which shows itself and says itself, which says itself in showing itself.

There is nothing to say: there is beginning, and thus, all at once, with a single stroke, in the white blank of title, the thing and the saying and their '*il y a*', their 'there is'. The 'there is' as the 'at once' of the thing and its saying. Meaning [*le sens*] as the meaning of being-there. There is no 'saying' this meaning, but there is saying and thing at the same time. The manisfestation is itself saying and thing together: utterance of a presentation, presentation of an utterance.

There is not the thing on the one hand and, on the other, the saying. The taking-place of the thing, its beginning-and-end, is at once saying and thing. It is the same 'thing': but a thing different in itself.

Consequently, therefore, it will be said this time: '*il y a blanc de titre*', 'there is white of title'. This time: that is, on the occasion of this painting by Susanna Fritscher. The occasion, the encounter, that which has neither beginning nor end, that which resides entirely in the instant, an interval [*battement*] between two series, between thing and saying, between place and place. The beating [*battement*] of an opening [*une ouverture*], as one speaks in the musical sense of an 'overture' [*une ouverture*][5]: a part in which the whole is restrained, in which the beginning takes its theme from the end, a cadence or a measure that withholds itself from succession, that does not take its measure from the ongoing, that breaks the continuation before it may continue.

'*Il y a blanc de titre*' is not a phrase any more than it is a silence. It is not a well-formed phrase; it lacks syntax and, as such, lacks meaning. But for all that, it is not a mystery, it does not hold some other meaning for the initiate, the visionary or the seer. It is a beginning – and who could be thus initiated at the beginning? It is, all at once, the beginning of a saying and of a thing, both of them white blanks in place of their titles: not indicating itself, not referring one to the other. Not making sense [*sens*], yet still saying what is full of sense: *voici, il y a*; look here, there is.

When there is a title, one of two things must have preceded it: either the thing-thing, within which something would have begun or initiated some meaning [*sens*] to be proposed, indicated or evoked; or else the thing-saying, within which some indication or signification from whence the thing could have taken its élan. But here, neither one has begun; both have finished together, at the intersection of a painting and an intention, at this intersection about which there is neither anything to paint nor anything to say, and which effects the opening of both things – or, rather, the opening of what separates them, namely, the very interplay of the intersection. It is precisely at this opening that each thing is opened *for* itself as *with* the other. It is open to the shared beat of a white blank of title.

'*Il y a blanc de titre*' does not act as a title in order to supplement the absence of a title given [*donné*] by Susanna Fritscher. (One should note that this could be read two ways: as either 'absence of a (given) title' or 'absence as title (given)'.[6] The fact that she will not have given a title can either amount to her keeping the title a secret, or to her having given absence and the white blank of title as a title. Perhaps painting always gives absence to the title, and writing a title to absence.

It is not a substitute for a title, nor a title by default. It indicates – but does not indicate; it exposes – but without showing, this absence itself as the beginning of the thing. The painting [*la peinture*; also, painting, paint] as beginning of the thing. The painting supervenes where titles end – at least if the function of a title is indeed to say exactly what this painting is, where it comes from, where it is going, what it means, what it wants to say. (But one knows, in fact, that it is nothing like this, and that titles never express [*disent*] anything except their own intersection with painting which, for its part, says nothing but only touches on the edge of titles, touching by its retreat. In this sense, all titles are white blanks, white blanks of painting. And the same is true for the titles of writings.)

'*Il y a blanc de titre*' does not replace some absent title. It neither evokes nor mimes any meaning which Susanna Fritscher or anyone else might have retained or detained. If it was, despite everything, to take the place of something, this could only be the place of the name of Susanna Fritscher. But in the place of a proper name, there is nothing; there is no place. The place of a proper name is itself only the space-time of a beginning, the spacing of a time, the time of a spacing: the birth of this woman.

'*Il y a . . .*', therefore, just as easily takes her place – by which I mean, the place of she who paints these canvases. The place, then, of her gesture of painting. Her gesture of touching canvas and paint, of touching canvas with paint, and of making paint touch itself, without beginning or end, right at the beginning and at the end of painting, sweeping itself along itself, sliding smoothly upon itself, by consenting layers layered one on the other, touching upon the without with the whole of its within.

Despite everything, it does also act as a title. For a title is neither a proper name, nor a common name. It does not signify, any more than it designates. The title is not a sign. On the contrary; the title is always a division [*un écart*], a gap [*un écartement*] within [*de*] the thing, the mark of a white space [*un blanc*] between the thing and itself: its very beginning and its end, the space by which it opens itself and stays open. The title says nothing: it indicates that everything is to be said, or nothing. The title does nothing but touch upon [*toucher à*; also, to tamper with] the closed thing, on the closure which it must have in order to open itself, in order that there be opening. The title closes and opens with a single gesture: it is the overture.

There is something: it begins, '*Il y a*' – 'there is' – the title itself; the title of every title and the white blank of the title. '*Il y a*' pertains at once to both the saying and to the thing, and reverts neither to one nor the other. '*Il y a*' is common to the saying and to the thing, which have nothing in common. It is between the two; it is, precisely, the in-between, the sharing [*le partage*; also, the division] of the saying and the thing. The to-and-fro of one to the other. Being in saying and the saying in being, the one outside the other, the one touching the other, the one beginning where the other finishes, the one beginning the other finishing the one.

Something reaches the edge of the saying, saying nothing, putting an end to the saying prior to which it began. A thing comes to speak of its own beginning, not speaking, putting an end to this beginning, beginning to be in this end. Neither cause nor production, reason or foundation to proceed from: only a gesture, a passage, a flow, sustained, smoothed, advanced and immobilised upon itself. Only a technique – that is to say, an art of brushing against the thing [*un art de passer à même la chose*], of passing into it, of passing through it, of coming from it into itself, continually, discretely, always at the limit, but at the limit deployed without limits.

We can call this: painting. The word gives a support but at

once poses an obstacle. What is it to paint? It is neither to represent, nor to cover a surface. It is to touch on an *il y a,* on a there is, on its absolute without end or beginning. A thing consents to being there: it occupies its place, it takes place there, it makes sense [*sens*] simply in order to open up this place. To paint is to consent to this consent. To paint is not to bespeak [*dire*] the event of this taking place, it is not the holding in check of signification. It is to consent to the division which deposes and exposes the thing.

It is the double movement of losing itself in itself and of opening itself to the outside: of losing itself in opening itself, of opening that which loses itself to its very loss. Its loss is its opening: it is not a loss, because nothing was gained or possessed. But to lose itself in itself *is* the opening. And it opens this: the thing itself to itself, layer upon staggered layer, interwoven in such a way that nothing is left but that presence which, in making a surface, thereby steals itself away. We could say that this opening appears [*paraît*]. It appears [*il apparaît*] rather, that there is appearing [*l'apparître*], and that this appearing has already returned into itself, already finished with appearing.

The opening opens nothing and opens onto nothing: neither density nor depth. Depth itself is a white blank. The opening at once opens what remains obstinately closed in the opening itself, and what is always already open, what is always already half-open. This is also why it finishes the beginning and begins the end. This has nothing to do with play, nor with verbal chatter. It is the opposing face of the verbal. It is the patience of consenting to being-there.

The grey yields to the white, which in turn yields to the grey, giving each other end and beginning, each giving itself to the other. From one to the other there is mixture and caesura, sharing, and that is all. But this sharing shares nothing distinct or allocated. It is not an exchange or a re-partition. It is a sharing of the same amongst the same, difference *per se,* distinction as common desire, common attraction. What draws one to the other and one out of the other is the community of their consenting to differ from one another. But consenting to differ in an imperceptible [*insensible*] way, because each one is nothing but the limit of the other. The other thus persists in the other, insensibly, indefinitely – yet losing itself therein.

Yet, how to consent to the insensible? How to have a sense [*avoir le sens*] of the insensible and, harmonising with it, thereby discover its rhythm? The insensible itself must be sensible, insensibly sensible: neither coldness, retreat or indifference, but in some way, the sensing [*le sentir*] itself, suspended on itself, opened onto itself. The grey-white interior of the act of sensing. In truth, one can say neither grey nor white, any more than one can speak here of 'support', 'surface', 'tableau', 'motif' or 'figure'. Grey and white are but the poles of this flow of light through which there is light (black is an other light, one which plays no role here: the light of truth, its abyss). Grey and white

are the-beginning-the-end of the appearing [*l'apparaître*]. Thus, there is within them only the discontinuity of continuity, the event of being: it is only event, and the event *is* not. Grey and white cannot be understood here as colours or as shades, or their combination or distillation. Colour is quite simply absent. There is nothing of the order of colour, in so far as colour is what belongs to a surface irrespective of its. Specifically, there are only dimensions. There is only measure and relation. Thus, since it is impossible to have a surface without colour, one can say that, here, there is no surface. Equally, one will say that there is pure depth, or that there is pure dimension. It is the same thing: there is opening, there is spacing. Like a stretch of water, at once opened and closed, in and upon itself.

Equally, from one frame of the diptych, triptych or monotype lay-outs to the next, and between these lay-outs, between these divisions [*découpes*] or between these statements [*relevés*], there is play and relation, continuity and discontinuity, time and counter-time, discretion of division [*l'écart*] and of touch [*le toucher*], imminence and contiguity. There is tact – or, in German, *Takt,* which is to say, cadence or measure.

There is measure, that is to say, relation and magnitude. The relation lies in affinity and in division, the magnitude lies in closure and distance. The measure is the cadence of one in the other, shadow and light, beginning and end. This measure is itself measureless. It surpasses all measure, it lies in the movement of this very surpassing, clear-cut, tenuous, like the passage and the sharing. The measureless measure is the consent to '*il y a*', to 'there is'. Not the acceptance of everything that there is, but consent to this 'there is' – and this latter is the measure or the rule for knowing what one must (or must not) accept.

It is the measure or the rule of what remains measureless: *the fact that there is* [*qu'il y a*]. What there is, all things, all this has colour and figure. But *the fact that there is,* is white and grey, is the-beginning-the-end of everything.

And if painting's verb was: to consent? Its verb, that is to say, its act; not its magic word, or its more or less sacred name, but, on the contrary, this absolute severing [*ce tranchant absolu*] of the verb upon the name, which breaks signification, which wrecks the referential constant? The referent of a name is a subject or a substance; the referent of an adjective is a quality of a substance and, precisely because of this, still substantial. But the referent of a verb is an action, which is not a state, or which is, at the very least, the action of maintaining the state, of persevering in being, when it is not the action of leaving being to itself, the action of existing or of exciting [*de l'exister ou de l'exciter*]. Action is always transitive. There is no intransitive verb. Perhaps – perhaps even above all – not even the verb 'to be'.

'To consent to': not to resign oneself, to submit, to concede through weariness or through passivity. Nor to enter into a 'consensus'. But to admit that there is a division – that of the anguish which you express [*tu dis*], of this anguish which everybody expresses and loses in expressing; and, nonetheless, no anguish, or anguish itself immediately opened into something other, become passage.

To consent to this: to one's own gesture, in so far as it goes without saying [*il va de soi*; literally, it goes from itself], goes much further or simply goes somewhere else to which no will would have been able to force it to go; and yet not abandoned – or if so, then abandoned in a very particular way: abandoned to one's own exactitude. Exactitude has nothing to do with precision. Precision approaches indefinitely; it is a matter of reproduction, of recuperation, of approximation. Exactitude is absolute or it is nothing. It is a matter of suddenly appearing, a matter of the instant.

It seems to me that we could say: we consent to exactitude. The exactitude of painting and that of writing are, assuredly, not the same – and there is, above all, no exactitude of one in respect of the other: no exact phrase 'on' painting, no exact painting 'on' the phrase. But, nonetheless, we all the same consent [*con-sentons*] to the same exactitude (that is to say, as we consent to it, we admit it together and in the same way).

We consent to exactitude because it is not something that one can command or master: one can only consent (and one can, in general, consent to this alone, to the exact). One cannot approach it. One can only *be here* [*y être*]. (However, all of the work [*travail*] consists in approaching it, while never approaching it, yet approaching nonetheless by a painstaking elimination of every attempt to approach. The patience of the painting is to disperse with every approach, so as to allow the thing to open up.)

Klee once said that to write and to design were the same thing. This is to speak from the point of view of exactitude while treating it nonetheless as an achieved proximity, as an extreme precision: it is therefore false. The truth of exactitude and of consent is that they are not the same thing, and that no art is the same as another (this is the price of 'art'). To consent to the exact: this would be for me, today, painting's word – as if it thus expressed the edge of writing, the edge of the trace of saying.

In fact, this amounts to 'saying' – in the sense that nothing should remain which is not said exactly, and that nothing exists which is not said exactly. For that which is not said does not exist, and that which is not said with exactitude is not said at all.

But to say with exactitude is go to right up to the limit of the saying – right up to its end, right up to its beginning. It is to put the finger of saying on the edge of painting. It is thus 'to be silent' or 'to silence oneself' – but in the exact sense where keeping something quiet, *being silent about it in painting*, is like saying this thing. Not saying it in another language, but saying it, very exactly, on the opposite face of language. Not saying it, then, but saying everything, saying everything about it, admitting it without reserve and without after-world.

What one thus calls painting would, from the first, be this (and this would also be the case with writing): it would be slipped into writing, right up to its extremity, more ancient in its gesture than its very gesture. This would be the water of writing, the water of ink, the ink which loses itself in its water, writing as the insensible limit of ink and of water.

You [*Tu*] must say that which you must keep silent. You must say it right up to the insensible, within the insensible itself. What, then, is this meaning [*sens*] which one no longer senses and which means [*sent*] no more than its own vanishing into obviousness? You must go on saying it right up to the extremity, right up to its excess and right up to the white blank, right up to the grey of saying. You must consent to saying everything, because everything is said. Everything is said because everything articulates itself from an *il y a*, from a 'there is'. But every *il y a*, every 'there is', expresses itself from a white blank, or expresses a blank – white-or-grey. Of everything that is said in this way, and which is the whole (of it), of everything that there is, there is no totality. Every *l'il y a*, every 'the there is', is, every time, here and now, each time spaced out of the whole, of all possible totality [*Tout l'il y a n'est que chaque fois, ici et maintenant, chaque fois espacé du tout, de toute totalité possible*]. *To* consent: to sense with. To sense each time *with* this time. To be on the threshold which separates this time from every other time, and which effects their relation, their common measure. To consent to this being, that is to say, to this step [*pas*] upon the threshold. To put this yet another way: to consent to sense the insensible opening of being-there, here and now.　　*Translated by Simon Sparks*

Notes

All footnotes have been added by the translator. I am indebted to Richard Stamp for reading an earlier version of this translation.

1 The title of Nancy's text, *Il y a un blanc de titre* is not as he points out, particularly 'well formed'. Its quasi-literal translation – '*There Is White [or Blank or Space] of Title*' – retains for an Anglophone ear precisely the same sort of grammatical violence wreaked upon a French ear by the original. But if, as Nancy says elsewhere, we are today suffering from a crisis of *sens* or meaning, then this lack of *sens* is perhaps the 'timeliest' aspect of this text. *Il y a blanc de titre*: this ill-formed phrase is dealt with in Nancy's text. One should, however, note several points not addressed explicitly:

(a) the French phrase ('*il y a*' literally, 'it has there'; colloquially. 'there is') has been traditionally used to translate Heidegger's term *es gibt* (literally, 'it gives', from the German verb *geben*, to 'give', more generally, 'there is'). In Heidegger's text, *es gibt* is interpreted as the event (*Ereignis*) of being, the gift through which 'there is' being. Nancy's use of *il y a* therefore names – at least partially – a form of essential questioning, that is, a form of questioning which attends to the question of the essence. Nancy's is not an art-critical account of a particular body or corpus of painting, but a philosophical (or, more recently ontological) account of that work. The '*Il y a*' marks the focus of this text as the impersonality, of the taking place 'itself'. The reader might consult with profit the text by Emmanuel Levinas. '*Il y a*' in *De l'existence à l'existents* [Vrin, Paris, 1947], translated as 'There is' in *From Existence to Existents*, Martinus Nijhoff, The Hague, 1978.

(b) *blanc*: this word has a multitude of extensions, and its translation in the title as 'white blank' attests, from the beginning, to the failure of this translation. *Blanc* can be taken, for example, as the masculine form of the adjective 'white' (having all the connotations of innocence, purity etc which are contained in the English word), but can also function as the noun 'blank', as in the term *tirer a blanc,* to fire blanks. Finally, however, and in the light of the typographical layout of Nancy's text (reproduced here) and the *agencements* or layouts of Fritscher's paintings, one needs to hear in the *blanc* a reference to Mallarmé and, in particular his *Préface to un coup de dés*, where 'the "spaces" (ie the white spacings of the blank page), indeed assume primary importance'. See Jacques Derrida, 'Mallarmé 'in *Tableau de la littérature française*, Gallimard, Paris, 1974, translated in *Acts of Literature*, Derek Attridge (ed), Routledge, London, 1992: 'the white of the spacing has no determinate meaning'. On the *blanc* in Mallarmé, see also Derrida's *La Dissémation,* Seuil, Paris, 1972, pp204-5, translated as *Dissemation*, University of Chicago Press, Chicago, 1981. There is a sense in which, at every moment, Nancy 'intends' a particular sense of the *blanc,* and one could translate accordingly; at the same time, however, Nancy's text can be read as a putting into play the ambiguities inherent in the *blanc,* at each moment gathering them together as *blanc,* refusing any 'final' decision. The translation has, then, tried to offer a range of possibilities (white blank, white space, blank space) which maintains Nancy's *sens,* rather than imposing any rigidly singular interpretation. (c) the phrase – *il y a un blanc de titre* – can be related to the grammatically exact model of the *il n'y a pas de titre,* the 'there is no title'. In rewriting the negation or the refusal of the title – the *ne pas* – in terms of *blanc,* Nancy complicates the relation between the title's absence and any polemological metaphysics of absence/presence. The *blanc* can perhaps be seen, then, as offering another way of contemplating the question of absence. As he writes below: 'There is not there, no over there, caught, lost, absent. There is no absence. Or better: there is absence itself in presence. It is for this reason that we cannot say we cannot say it'.

2 Throughout, Nancy uses the verb *dire* (rather than *parler, addresser* etc) in order to express the relation between the articulation of the event (double genitive), what will be called saying (*son dire*), and its sense (*vouloir dire*) or meaning (*sens*). This has almost always been rendered by the verb to say and its cognates, expecting those instances where the English syntax, unlike the French is abused. The French has been noted in square brackets in such cases.

3 Here, as elsewhere in this text, Nancy declines a verb as a noun. Each time this takes place, a certain active sense needs to be ascribed to this new term: ie, it is a case of the noun functioning both to name the act of something happening as well as giving itself a transitive force.

4 The verb *consentir* – whose resonances with *sentir* (to sense or feel) and *sens* (sense or meaning) and all this latter's derivations, need to be borne in mind – has consistently been translated as either 'to yield' or 'to consent', depending on context.

5 As Nancy here makes clear, the idea of the *ouverture* between the place of the thing (the painting etc) and the place of the saying, needs to be understood both in relation to the action of opening (in French, *ouvrir*) and to the musical sense of an introduction, to or opening of, a cantata. The translation of *ouverture* – consistently either by opening or by *ouverture*, depending on the context – has each time an interpretative force, and the unity of the terms in French should be borne in mind.

6 This double reading – or, as is said in French, double writing (*cela . . . peut s'écrire de deux manières*) – cannot be translated adroitly. Nancy plays upon the agreement of the word 'given' (*donné(e)*) with either *le titre* (masculine) or *l'absence* (feminine) to complicate the status of the title's absence. The text reads: '*ou bien "l'absence de titre donné", ou bien "l'absence de titre donnée"* '.

Susanna Fritscher, FROM ABOVE, PAGE 28: Exposition Credac, *Paris, April 1994; Exposition Galerie E Manet, Paris, September 1994 (photos, Laurent Lecat)*

ART AND ART HISTORY IN THE NEW MUSEUM
THE SEARCH FOR A NEW IDENTITY

Hans Belting

The following essay considers the fate of the museum in an age of information that has redetermined the status of art objects today. If the classical museum functioned as keeper of timeless and universal Enlightenment values, the contemporary art museum now plays an entertainment-oriented role. Theatricality becomes the hallmark of the new museum, in which the orchestration of temporary exhibitions stimulates the myth of cultural stability. Within the space of carefully designed exhibitions, likened to telematic 'screen environments', Belting surmises that such events supplant actual artworks. As museums move into the information age, attended to by the immaterial image, the identity of art history as anchored within the museological edifice must undergo profound reconsideration. 'The question,' Belting asks, 'is not whether the contemporary museum should exist, but rather, whether the traditional museum and its task of historical representation is still at all possible'. DM

The site where the development of art history takes place today, and will do so in future, is the contemporary art museum. It is not simply a place for exhibiting contemporary art, but also a site for displaying our ideas on the history of art. It is precisely in this area that questions have arisen as to whether the idea of seeing history of art mirrored in contemporary art is still of general value, if it can exist at all. The many diverging concepts of art today raise questions about whether we can have a mutual understanding of art history that can be displayed in our museums in an unproblematical manner. It is inadequate simply to display works of art that cannot embody an idea of the development of art history and the position of art. We are still shackled to an idea of 'art' that is increasingly more difficult to understand. We can only identify it in the context of the course it has taken up until the present, whatever our concept of history may be.

The museum, as a site where a discussion about the autonomy of artists and art experts is taking place, is at the moment also being questioned by people who have diverging opinions. The museum, subjected to public pressure, should be able to display all that books are no longer capable of explaining, and the question of content has for some time no longer been solely a matter for the experts. There are no debates about the museum that are not also debates about the idea of art history. In areas where this idea has become uncertain, one takes a positive initiative and leaves the field open to the most diverse ideas in order to keep face in some fashion. When there is no longer any consensus in art, any kind of art can demand to be seen in a museum. If a museum cannot incorporate all of the demanded criteria, it can help itself by holding changing exhibitions. In this manner, all irreconcilable expectations can be met by allowing a maximum number of diverse ideas to be expressed one after the other.

The institution itself benefits from the controversies concerning the contents of displays and activities. Therefore, it will still be able to play its former role in a variety of disguises in the immediate future. When the Museum of Modern Art opened the exhibition *High and Low* in New York in 1990, it presented itself with a new look opposed to the ideals of the hallowed temple of Classical Modernism. Complaints about the 'desecration of the temple' ensued, as the institution appeared to have incorporated the vulgar design of advertising. The museum as a *temple* of art instead of a *school* is still a concept dating from the bourgeois era, as Arthur C Danto stated in this context, although it sanctified Modernism, of all things, in this particular case. As late as 1958, Ad Reinhardt strongly campaigned for the museum as 'shrine' and against the museum as a site for recreation. Three years later, Claes Oldenburg tuned the tables and exchanged the shrine for a shop in his *Store Manifesto*.

The contemporary museum has failed to turn into a department store although, in the meantime, it uses all available techniques of advertising to show controversial forms of art in the most advantageous manner. The main task of the institution, that appears more and more like theatre with its ever changing programme, is to create an original setting. To use another comparison, goods of the most diverse origins can find a 'free trade zone', where a symbolic bid for acceptance by the art scene is made. The question often arises whether it is new art that is looking for the context of a museum, or whether the museum is in fact looking for new art. Contemporary art would not only be homeless without the museum, it would also be voiceless and invisible. The museum, on the other hand, despite being badly prepared for contemporary art, would become antiquated if it closed its doors to it. This forced alliance therefore automatically annihilates any alternatives to the museum.

It was possible to speak of a 'crisis of the museum' in the 70s, just as there was a discussion of a crisis of art. In the meantime, this crisis concerning meaning has been replaced by the boom of the museums. The design ideas of the organisers and the public's wish for entertainment have been satisfied to such an extent that these eternal questions are gradually no longer being posed. Any person can now decide things for himself or herself. The 'widening out' of the museum, in demand for such a long time, is proceeding at full pace but has taken on a different form than was expected. Instead of providing a democratised art for a wide public, the museum itself continues to fall increasingly into the hands of this public. The public puts itself on show against the backdrop of this aesthetic island, after having lost the public framework for any other public appearances.

As early as 1980, Douglas Crimp had a sensuously destructive vision of himself sitting *On the Museum's Ruins,* the title of a contribution to the magazine *October.* He had in mind the ruins of the illusion of the museum, displaying art as a homogeneous system and history of art as its ideal structuring system. His criticisms inflamed the prevalent 'moral and aesthetic autonomy' of modern art. Crimp found this incompatible with the demands of his Marxist idea of representation, as he wished to force modern art as an illustration of society. He would have loved to proclaim an archaeology of the museum which would expose it as an ancient place of asylum for art existing in an airtight vacuum. He complained of the 'neo-conservative use of the museum as a site of the beaux arts' and, in another essay, called for resistance to a false post modernism, that rediscovers ancient genealogies in art, 'returning to an unbroken continuum of museum art'.

Meanwhile, the wheel of history has turned yet again and has robbed so-called museum art of the exclusivity Crimp disliked, even if there are enough attempts to keep the temple pure. In this way, the old controversies disappear un-problematically, hailing the dawning of a new era. Museum art no longer has an exclusive image with which it can occupy a privileged and alternative site. This was only possible as long as artists were successfully excluded from the museum. Today, museum art includes everything, as everything can be found standing or hanging in a museum. With gratitude, museums submissively accept the most unsuitable private collections, subjected to the all-powerful dictates of the donor.

At the same time, a trend toward contemporaneity has become greater and is described by S Gohr as a return to the yearly *Salon* of the 19th century. Contradictions in our culture are expressed in the ambiguous relationship between museum and art fair. For some time it has no longer been possible to assign the museum to culture and the art fair solely to the market, as our culture so willingly pledges itself to the dominance of museum policies and the principles of marketing. The goods that are traded at the art fair are simultaneously consecrated by the museum. There is, however, more to this problem. Institutions and public rituals take over all areas where art is no longer considered as possessing any strength to convince of its own. By means of increased communication, the customary prestige of art that has become weakened is fortified by the enlargement of institutional spaces. Society, for the most diverse

reasons, needs a culture of prestige and is therefore convinced it must give art credit, without taking into consideration what it has in fact achieved.

Prices serve as advertisements for cultural status and often hinder the purchase of a work of art by the same museum that unwittingly brought this about by means of its exhibition policies. They naturally follow the laws of the market and an impression that art has been reduced to exchange goods, speculated with by anyone wishing to invest money, is brought about much too rapidly. The legendary prices that have also been achieved by living artists must, however, also been seen in another light. They are also the tangible symbols of an old myth about art that is today only expressed in figures which gain an aura that the art itself has largely lost. Such prices bring forth an astonishment that is actually meant for art, but which it is often unable to bring about itself. They contribute to the remythologising of art, which people are as reluctant to lose as the religion that has already been lost.

Works of art in museum collections, that no longer have any market value, are 'displayed' on the changing stage of the museum so that they constantly appear in a new light. The stage, on which contemporary exhibition techniques are rehearsed, belongs to a theatre, with its modern museum architecture that now competes successfully with theatres and concert halls. The presentation of art begins with the exterior of the building and its inviting gestures, and continues with the exhibition spaces that are constantly rearranged like a stage. If the presentation itself is insufficient, 'museum education' comes to the fore, having appealed to a new public for the last 20 years. As is the case with the presentation of the museum, this does not appeal solely to the 'opening up' of the temple, but is a reaction to the crisis in 'art as religion', thus strengthening the trend towards secularisation that has been on the agenda for a long time.

The boom in museum construction validates itself with an expressive aesthetic will for which there are no longer any architectural tasks and therefore the actual function of the museum is lost. Museum architecture in Germany was discovered as the latest architectural task suitable for the 'applied art of building', as A Preiss wrote in an informative volume of essays about the contemporary museum. The museum represents the cultural state or cultural city which can no longer express itself convincingly in other ways. Its representative qualities are more effective than those of opera houses and concert halls with their high ticket prices. Moreover, it remains unhampered by the contradictions inherent in the admiration of a bourgeois culture, although we are no longer a bourgeois society.

After entering the art theatre, we are greeted by a rich variety of exhibitions that fulfil two very different wishes In a masterful fashion: the wish for information and the wish to be amused. The wish to be informed is brought about by the lack of insight into the contemporary art scene where everyone has lost track. Exhibitions now dominate all other communications about the state of the art and the development of the history of art. They had always had their function when a new movement wished to attract attention in the form of what amounted to a manifesto. Today, however, they fill the gaps in a world of information that can only be filled by statements, by works of art that demonstrate these statements.

The ritualistic aspects of art, the roots of which we know little about, gain all the more significance with a public lacking in experts. They astound such a public with effects that block any possible doubts in a single work of art. The enjoyment of an exhibition replaces the uncertain enjoyment of its exhibits. The new, aggressive exhibition technique is a reaction to the visual demands of a wider public, looking for a high standard of leisure entertainment that the media is increasingly unable to provide. Formerly, people went to museums to see objects that their grandparents had already seen in the same place, while today we visit museums to see something that has never been there before.

At the same time, the museum envelopes the visitor invitingly; its audiovisual atmosphere exposing a single visual impression, removed from his or her ordinary surroundings. The lighting in a dark spatial cell can simulate the intimacy between viewer and image, such as that which occurs in front of a television set. It is like a screen environment if we allow ourselves to be hypnotised for a while. The museum presents itself as a freely invented 'site of the imagination', replacing the unique and temple-like 'site of education' it formerly embodied. At the same time, it accommodates itself to an experience of space that has lost its corporeality – this occurs with the television set, where simple images remove themselves from space and then immediately reattach themselves. Consequently, we expect to find the simulation of telematic space in the museum that will immediately lead us out of the museum once again. The museum has become the railway station for the departing trains of the imagination, instead of the goal of a pilgrimage to the site of art. The installation also invents an alternative site within the museum, denying the memory of the museum as a site. The traditional museum stands in stark contrast to the destruction of space in our visual fantasy.

The museum was always the privileged shrine of a collection of originals that only a single site on earth possessed. The power of the present was also broken here and swapped for the time-scale of history. The museum thus lay outside the time of the visitor, while still remaining within the spatial experience of their bodies. The situation of temple and church was secularised, so that believers could experience mythical time spatially and physically: the cult images in this place were usually old but still visible and present as physical images, although there was only a single copy and therefore a single site that had to be reached. The museum, symbolising a permanent and timeless site, is therefore at odds with all those contemporary wishes that are articulated in contemporary exhibition trends with their ephemeral character. A society that honours a database of information instead of a collection of objects needs a new strategy in museums in order to remove space and add time. The 'event' replaces the work of art.

New settings, however, have their limits when traditional art, with its quality of immutability, is asked to provide sensationalism. In this case, museums call upon well-known 'guest curators' who are granted a period of freedom, not yet possessed by local staff. Recently, the third person in such a threesome could be found in Rotterdam; Robert Wilson attempted to transform the museum into an actual stage upon which the 'performed' works from the museum collection could no longer be recognised. In a short while, a theatre in the Baroque spirit was created, engorged and then spewed out by history of art, as embodied by the traditional works of art in a glittering performance. The three static art forms – portrait, still life and landscape (this was the title of Robert Wilson's exhibition) – simultaneously provided the repertoire of scripts for the 'scenic' performance, although even the most open-minded viewer would find a Rodin bronze in an artificially lit autumn forest entitled *Still Life* rather contrived. There is a treacherousness in allowing a stage director to work in a museum, giving him a historical stage with historical props for a guest production.

In 1993, the same year in which Wilson created theatre in a museum, Peter Greenaway showed a film in another museum, or rather, created the situation of a film without actually filming. The setting was the eccentric art collection of the former theatre designer, Mariano Fortuny, in Venice, a place in which statues, masks, porcelain and old materials transform themselves into the props of an imaginary show and are integrated with the actual paintings of the collector. The filmmaker was inspired by the idea of creating an exhibition entitled *Watching Water*, in which he showed props from his films. As in the traditional collection, with its appearance of being designed for the worship of cultural memories, he erected floodlights from a film studio that lit up parts of the collection, lit up figures in the paintings or let them disappear into the dark, according to an invisible scheme. The viewer thought he was part of a film, taking part in it himself, with the co-actors in the collection waiting silently for him to wake up to his short life on stage. In an interview published in the *Film Bulletin* in June 1994, Greenaway expressed a wish to 'overcome the cinematic situation' and bring the public back to space and corporeality which it had lost with the ersatz of the cinema screen. His projects, including a travelling exhibition entitled *100 objects to represent the world* culminated in the exhibition *Stairs,* which transformed the whole city of Geneva into a stage. The viewer could create a cinematic situation himself from a hundred geographical sites, reached via steps, by experiencing the world as a stage with all the coincidences of the passing moment, looking through a frame that is the equivalent of the frame of a cinema screen with his own eyes. The world, art and film merged to create a theatrical situation in which the viewer played a role.

The art exhibition is now increasingly being transformed into a spectacle by theatrical directors, who are also art historians, and are not capable of understanding an aesthetic spectacle. There are already exhibitions in which older and newer works react against one another in the form of false or playful genealogies that appear to be liberated from the laws of art history. We are coerced into making original comparisons in order to convince us of a freshly constructed thesis. The experiments, however, are still limited to temporary exhibitions in which they also reach far beyond such perspectives. In the last version of the *Sonsbeek* exhibition in Arnhem in 1993, the American artist, Valerie Smith, constructed a hermaphrodite, incorporating a cabinet of wax figures and a country fair in which the promiscuity of old and new, of art and eccentric artefacts had a disorientating effect. The traditional cabinet of curiosities, which was the forerunner of the museum, was reborn, with contemporary works of art, stuffed animals and kitsch statues of saints from museum depots. Any thoughts concerning art and art history appeared absurd in this atmosphere of dust and make-up because the spectacle unleashed a chaos of images and comparisons without exciting the wonder people formerly experienced in the microcosm of the 'cabinet of curiosities'. Contemporary works of art appeared to be robbed of their power as living art in this vicinity, as if they were also part of the depot of our cultural memory.

The pre-museum 'cabinet of curiosities', to which Horst Bredekamp draws our attention, appears where machines and art, after whose separation the museum was created, come together again in media art. An exhibition by the American media artist, Gary Hill, in the new Kunsthalle Wien, now standing around like a forgotten container on the Karlsplatz, required such complicated technology that specialists had to work on it for several weeks. At the opening, the electrical gear, similar to that of the electronic plant behind the stage of the theatre, was hidden so well that the illusion of technical images without technology was created. The exhibition only existed as long as the electricity was turned on, because it was when the monitors were turned on that the dark spatial cells were lit up and filled by video images. Immaterial visual spaces, furnished for a certain period of time, were created in the existing architectural structures; they could neither be photographed, nor described in words and therefore exhibition catalogues could no longer provide an image. The earlier presence of the works of art, with their laws of durability, are here replaced by the presence of a viewer who enters a room like this for a moment and can then only remember the impression he formed himself. The brief first impression replaces an enduring original and the objects on view are reduced to the functionality of 'hardware'. The art that is exhibited in such a fashion is dependent on the technology it is created by and the computer organises the imagery of the video-tapes during the period of viewing.

Presently, the computer reigns over the old contrast between technology and spirit as a post-technical instrument of the imagination. Its iconography, bringing a calculated (and not an analogous) world to the screen, eliminates the differences between image and sign in a mixture of imagery and technology. The computer therefore presents a challenge to traditional ideas of creative art forms that have found a false answer in what are termed computer graphics. It also leads to new ideas about the role of the museum because it can save everything by robbing all the objects formerly collected (and exhibited) in museums of their corporeal existence. Museums and computers are therefore at odds with one another. The experience of place, in which the corporeal objects stand, takes place in the museum and it is the experience of the time from which they date that is communicated by the exhibits. The images in a computer are presented in a manner removed from space and time and are converted into pure information.

The collecting policy of the museum and the collecting possibilities of the computer belong to diverse ages, although they exist alongside one another in the present. The collecting policies of the art museum, unlike collections of natural history and technology, are based on the principle of selection and the validity of what we describe as 'art'. This principle led to the great divide of images and objects created by man in former times. Images within the museum gained the status of art, while all images outside its walls simultaneously lost this credibility. In this manner, we are coming into an old inheritance that we can only attribute with sense in a contemporary manner with great difficulty, even if there cannot be any doubts about their former meaning.

As we know, art was an idea from the age of the Enlightenment which attributed to it timelessness and universality, beyond all the differences between individual artistic processes: as timeless and universal as Common Human Rights, that should apply to all humans, although the individuals differ to a great extent. This idea of art could only be kept alive if combined with an idea of the history of art. The time of history of art, however, considered itself more important than the individual time of the works of art, and history of art was universally applicable in a manner not possible for individual works. Therefore a place was invented where all individual art was part of the general principle of art: the art museum. Here, only that which could represent history of art could be accepted and this was only older art, as can already be seen with the founding of the Louvre, while new art could only earn the status of museum art and was therefore placed on a waiting list.

The nervousness that always appears when contemporary art is defined in an unambiguous manner, often demonstrates that we are still bound to an idea that is merely two hundred years old, regardless of the age of the works of art to which it is applied. We are undoubtedly interested in keeping up the connection with the great tradition of historical culture, as it would be a fatal loss if art only belonged to the past. The crux of the matter is that we can only define contemporary art with this ancient principle of art. Therefore we must use the horizons of its history: only this history can explain what cannot actually be explained in words. Art that is created today automatically has a particular privilege that pure ideas cannot have: it can be bought as a work of art, with a creator and a price, by a museum and exhibited there as a work of art. Although it is in actual fact an idea, it is given form by works of art that always have a place and name of their own. Even if this is only an illusion, as M Duchamp guessed, it is a necessary illusion in which culture is given form. The ideal and material value belong together in a paradoxical manner, so that the material value has become autonomous through the daily practices of the art market. Although the art market defends sales values and the museum proclaims ownership, it is only the symbolic value that can win our attention.

In order to understand this symbolic value, that was visualised so obviously in art museums, it is of interest to re-examine the traditional role of the museum as a witness of history and as a cult site for a wider middle-class public. History, if it is at all possible, is shared history in which a community is drawn together, both in its positive and negative aspects. However, what is the situation in the art museum where this has such a contradictory existence and where many works of art pay for acceptance in the collections with the loss of their previous history in order to count as art in any manner? History, therefore, could not only be found in the evidence of individual works of art but rather in the evidence of an institution that presented itself as the property of everyone. The nation had replaced religion; the national museum, the former cathedral (which had taken over some objects from the former as a result of expropriation). Curiously enough, history received a new sense of authority behind museum doors because it triumphed over time with its 'immortal works of art' and also because the nation applauded itself as being its owner. In the museum, the works of art reached a terminal station in which time was immaterial. They are removed from the art market in order to be honoured in the name of history or the name of the art that history brings to the fore.

The art museum was embedded firmly in modern democracy, where it administered historical culture and art that had been transformed into history in the name of the state. It appears to belong to us all and still, or because of this, we do not have the right to take over the 'Temple of Art', at whose entrance the state has placed its watchmen. The subject (history of art) and its representative carriers (the national state) both come into view and this task of representation is also recognised today in the areas where contradictions sometimes appear in the museum programme. The National Gallery in Berlin was courageous enough to show a small number of works from their huge collection of 20th-century art by established artists from former East Germany, such as Willi Sitte and Wolfgang Mattheuer, in 1994. The outcry raised in the press was enormous, as if people were insulted by works of art smuggled into the historical consciousness that were negative for the honour of the nation. The idea of changing to a new normality without commentary was certainly wrong and was only made worse by a mistake with the dates of acquisition, as if there had never been two institutions carrying the same name, without making further information uniform. It must, however, have been surprising how much emotion could be raised by paintings whose place on public walls did not appear to be justified. The question of representation, that national identity is supposed to lead to, is a question concerning the institution and not a question of individual artistic achievement.

Verification is only possible if we follow the most recent developments in the former Socialist countries, where there is neither an innocent tradition of the museum, nor a secure and democratic state consciousness. The Party, in the name of the State, had taken away works of art from the Church and placed them in museums by means of forced nationalisation. After the unification of Germany, the Church wanted these back, once again wishing to expropriate museums that had existed under false labels. In Poland and Russia, the Church demanded the return of carved Gothic wooden altarpieces because it considered itself to be the true owner and inheritor of history. The ownership of the ancient *Icon of Vladimir* – whose honorary title was carried by a *Patroness of the Fatherland,* was the cause of a new disagreement between the Russian State and the Church and President Yeltzin – followed the example of Solomon, making the decision that it belonged to the State but could be used by the Church for services when needed. This process is interesting in many ways, as not only the right of ownership of the museums, but also the value of a work of art in favour of the more ancient ritual value, is being questioned. The example to the contrary is interesting. The memorials of Marx, Lenin and other party leaders, who were meant to represent the official *Weltanschauung*, as well as the State, are disappearing into hastily created open-air museums, if they have not already been destroyed, as if museums were places where history no longer has any power. This is the manner in which religious artefacts were dealt with 200 years ago, although people were convinced that they were dealing with works of art.

Today in the West, it is not the museum as such, but the contemporary museum, that raises doubts about its own role and appearance. It is looking for its own identity and is at the moment still clinging to that of the traditional museum although it has developed in another direction. In order to be taken seriously as an institution, its appearance is styled to look like the traditional institution and also has the questionable aim of exhibiting history of art, although this only concerns works of art that possess an uncertain genealogy in an art historical sense. The question is not whether the contemporary museum should exist, but rather whether the traditional museum and its task of historical representation are still possible. They have long since been transformed into an art centre with contemporary goods and rotating stages for the disconnected art world, yet have the false need to catalogue and canonise everything they have in order to make official history of art, whereby they also serve the art market that is reliant on the role of the museum.

The crisis of the institution that we are speaking of is here combined with a crisis within the public, as forum and carrier of opinion. Looking back at the history of the museum, the readiness of a bourgeois elite – consisting of art collectors and civil servants, wishing to celebrate a common ideal of art and ownership – becomes apparent. It was also the willingness to be represented as a cultural nation at a single site belonging to everyone, by a single idea of art and art history, therefore transferring collective identity to an institution chosen for this task and looking for this in the mirror of history: the history of national art schools and the traditional artistic objects of mankind. Not only is a diverging relationship towards history emerging, but also a different attitude to the public is becoming obvious at the present moment. A common culture is now being questioned just as much as the ability to develop a common consciousness, although a degree of tolerance provides some equilibrium. Additionally, there is finally the experience that everyone can present themselves publicly on a screen without having to be at a public place.

In the case of a museum in which the private initiative of individual collectors has always played a role, the sponsors increasingly wish to be represented personally and this diminishes collective representation. The Museum Ludwig in Cologne is the most spectacular example of this, if measured by the contrasting example of the Foundation of Prussian Cultural Property, Berlin. The wish to gain recognition expressed by individual collectors is supported by the recognition that the contemporary museum is a place for public activity in which not only exhibitions but film evenings, lectures and congresses can take place. To put it another way, a forum for communication exists that has become unique in its own way. The same public finally enters the museum with the wish to gain cultural information for which the popularisation of television no longer provides possibilities. On a cultural level, it is also looking for representation of its own time, for which it no longer possesses any appropriate symbols. We wish to construct an image of the present which was formerly offered by the latest developments of a unified history of art. We are perhaps also disappointed because the museum cannot fulfil our needs any longer, due to reasons that are all too obvious.

In the future we will probably have further symbols that still go under the label of art, but will liberate themselves from the context of education and historical culture, that formed the backbone of art until the present moment. The official culture was bound to a dominant discussion for so long and was, at the same time, marketed to such an extent that it no longer possesses the authority of a common ideal. For a long time, there has been a general wish no longer to leave the monopoly of self-expression in the hands of the artists while they, in turn, attempt to take over the 'Artists' Museums' themselves and liberate themselves from the market (Lodz). Newly created subjects call for symbols of communication that are no longer dominated by the dictates of a recognised artistic style (and its market value) in a regional and half-private framework. New tales and arguments are also created in art literature that does not wish to make concessions to a single 'history of art'. The exploding variety of the world is mirrored in a corresponding diversity of 'world images' that are, however, hindered by a monopolised media culture. Therefore, there is an increasing trend in the Western democracies to create a highly diverse, non-official culture in which traditional artistic value is just as uncertain (or unimportant) as the information value within the system of official 'history of art'.

Public attention was drawn to the Museum of Modern Art in New York and the 'Modernists' who visited it like a church, like members of the same persuasion congregating to hold a religious service. Its opponents, which included D Crimp, therefore rebelled vehemently against its wish 'to tell the story of modern art,' as he put it in 1984, in the name of all nonbelievers. They regarded its belief in the 'essence' of autonomous art (as formulated by the art critic Clement Greenberg) as a complete falsehood that could no longer be combined with the realities of artistic production and its contradictions, and therefore formed a programme that survived due to the beliefs of its adherents. Arthur C Danto, who belongs amongst the adherents, found himself forced to conclude that modernist 'history of art has come to an end' because it has fulfilled its aims. The 'end of modernism,' according to Greenberg, is, to be exact, 'the end of a theory that explains why art is high when it is high. What has come to an end is a certain concept of the history of art'.

This can be like a butterfly hunt, if one wishes to catch the 'image' of history of art that we have mentioned. Why do we need it if all artists, past and present, have proved themselves so obviously real, as real as history is, even if their works of art exist in reality in the same manner that objects exist? It is only possible to object to ideas that have also made history and that were given a material form. Art is a historical illusion, as Marcel Duchamp has proved, and so is art history, as André Malraux discovered inadvertently when he wrote about the *Museum Without Walls*. It is therefore a question of institutions, and not a question of contents, and certainly not a question of the methods by which art and the history of art will survive in future. The cathedrals have fairly recently finally outlived the founding of museums. Why shouldn't contemporary museums outlive the founding of other institutions in which history of art no longer has a recognisable place? *Translated by Flora Fischer*

THE SHAPE OF MEANING
WORD AND IMAGE IN A 15TH-CENTURY BOOK

James H Marrow

Medieval works of art, no less than contemporary ones, address basic issues of meaning and interpretation. Such concerns are readily visible in hand-produced books, where form, format, words and images articulate content, focus attention and structure experience and understanding. This essay treats a little-known medieval manuscript, which stands out as an exceptional exercise in the construction of meaning through a broad and sophisticated range of formal inventions. The original design of this book contradicts the conventional view of medieval manuscripts as the products of a scribal culture attuned to copying and resistant to real innovation. The book's singularity is the more noteworthy when one considers its sacred subject matter and its status as a representative of a manuscript type created more than a century before this exemplar was made. As we shall see, its creators purposefully reshaped the type so as to bring out new dimensions of its subject matter and alter its users' consciousness of their experience of the book's meaning.

The manuscript that concerns us is a *Biblia Pauperum* ('Pauper's Bible'), produced at the turn of the 15th century in the Northern Netherlands.[1] The *Biblia Pauperum* is the modern name for a type of book that sets forth the story of the redemption of mankind by Christ in the context of pertinent prophecies and prefigurations from the Old Testament.[2]

In the illustrated versions that dominate the tradition of copies of this book, a series of representations of important events from the New Testament (ranging from the Incarnation through Christ's Passion and the events associated with the Last Judgment and the end of time), are each accompanied by portrayals of four bust-length prophets and the texts of their prophecies referring to the event, and of two narrative incidents from the Old Testament that prefigure it. Composed probably around the mid-13th century in the region of present-day Austria or Southern Germany, the *Biblia Pauperum* enjoyed notable success. More than 80 manuscript copies survive in complete or fragmentary form, ranging in date from the turn of the 14th to the late-15th century. These are supplemented by editions printed both in blockbooks and moveable type, testifying to the enduring repute of the book in the era of printing.

From all evidence, the *Biblia Pauperum* was created in monastic circles and enjoyed its greatest popularity in this sphere. Summarising the course of Redemption in word and picture, placing it in the context of biblical history from the creation to the end of time, and illustrating the coherence of the two testaments, the *Biblia Pauperum* provided fitting material for instruction and edification. In the two and a half centuries of its currency, it underwent continuous evolution and development, circulating not only in its original Latin form but also in vernacular versions, appearing in cycles of different length and varying content, and taking different forms both in its layout and the style of its illustrations.[3]

The Golden *Biblia Pauperum*

Created more than a century after the invention of the *Biblia Pauperum*, the manuscript we shall treat (London, British Library, Kings Ms 5) is the most exceptional copy in the known tradition of this book. Termed the 'Golden *Biblia Pauperum*' because of the opulent technique of its pictures, the manuscript departs from all earlier copies of this text in its format and layout, the colours of its script, the luxurious technique of its illustrations, their subjects, sequence, expressive style and iconography.

To begin, earlier illustrated versions of the *Biblia Pauperum* are all in larger and vertically oriented books, taller than they are wide, and they are illustrated exclusively with pen or pen-and wash sketches arranged in schematic or diagrammatic configurations (*fig 1*). In contrast to the earlier copies, whose relatively economical pictorial technique, large size, and schematic forms reflect their use primarily for communal purposes in monasteries, the 'Golden *Biblia Pauperum*' is courtly in its opulent materials and appears to have been designed for private rather than communal use. The illustrations are executed as richly coloured, independently framed miniatures on highly decorated and burnished gold grounds, rather than in pen or pen-and-wash, and the script is written, uniquely, in alternating passages of blue, red, and gold, rather than brown.

As opposed to all earlier copies of the *Biblia Pauperum*, which open to reveal one or two full ensembles of subjects per page, Kings Ms 5 was originally arranged and bound not in its present-day oblong format (*figs 2, 5*), but as a series of 31 unusually folded leaves (*fig 3*). The leaves were folded twice along vertical axes flanking the central miniature and were sewn individually at the left fold. In its original folded form,

Kings Ms 5 was therefore comparable in size and shape to traditional books of private devotion, such as Psalters or Books of Hours.

The novel structure of the book, which appears to be unique, also has a devotional purpose, requiring that it be manipulated in a manner unlike that of conventional codices and thereby setting forth the content of each of the ensembles in a sequential process. At each folded ensemble, the reader first encountered a leaf containing only a rubricated title for the New Testament event that was to follow, although, by transparency, he could usually see some faint outlines of what lay behind the leaf (*fig 3*). Turning the first page he then found one Old Testament prefiguration on its verso and the blank side of a folded leaf on the facing recto, although here again there was usually some inkling of more to come in the dim outlines of forms showing through the blank side of the page. With the subject of the rubric not yet visible, but only prefigured in the first Old Testament event, the reader was then forced to uncover the folded recto leaf in order to reveal all three miniatures which make up each ensemble, that is, an event from the Christian scheme of Redemption flanked by two of its prefigurations from the Old Testament.

The unconventional structure of Kings Ms 5 leads its reader through a three-stage progression from expectation to fulfilment. With his anticipation aroused by the rubric of each ensemble, and then further stimulated when the first page is turned to reveal one Old Testament prefiguration, the reader has to take a third step and uncover the folded leaf in order to see the complete grouping and discover what had only been announced in each of the first two openings. The design of the book simulates the course of sacred history, both through the series of New Testament events it records and, as is unique to this copy, within the configuration of each ensemble. Demanding of the reader an unusual manipulation of the leaves of the volume, and thus drawing him in novel ways into the experience of the book, the structure of Kings Ms 5 heightens the meaning of the *Biblia Pauperum* as a document of the purposeful, evolutionary relationship between the two testaments. In turning and opening up the leaves which make up each folded ensemble, the reader is encouraged to envision sacred history as a literal 'unfolding' of the divine order as it progresses from the Old

Law to and through the New. The design of Kings Ms 5 thus articulates the content of the *Biblia Pauperum* in a radically original manner, giving new depth and resonance to its prophetic and redemptive message by altering the reader's sense of temporal engagement with the book.

Another unique feature of this copy of the *Biblia Pauperum* is its coloured script, which alternates passages of gold, blue, and red (*figs 2, 3*). In addition to registering its courtly qualities, the coloured script of Kings Ms 5 seems to me to evoke particular traditions for characterising sacred texts. We may recall, for example, the use of rich, coloured pigments for scripts in biblical manuscripts, such as the numerous 'golden Gospel books' and 'golden Psalters' of the Hiberno-Saxon, Carolingian, and Ottonian eras. This tradition extends even into the 14th century, for the Gospel Book of Johannes von Troppau, a Bohemian manuscript of 1368, is written throughout in gold script complemented by blue chapter headings and capital letters alternating red and blue.[4]

One other tradition may be echoed in the coloured scripts of Kings Ms 5, namely, that of liturgical calendars, some of which are written in graded and decoratively arranged patterns of gold, red, and blue script. Inasmuch as the *Biblia Pauperum* outlines the course of sacred history, much as does the liturgy itself, it seems possible that in choosing gold, red, and blue pigments for its script, the designer of Kings Ms 5 meant to evoke the sacral and festive character of liturgical calendars, if not also their function in summarising the unfolding scheme of sacred time.

The coloured pigments of the script in Kings Ms 5 likely function also as basic aesthetic analogues of the structure and meaning of the *Biblia Pauperum*. Every ensemble of the *Biblia Pauperum* is simultaneously made up of triadic and dyadic groupings. That is, while each ensemble consists of three narrative illustrations, at the same time, it illustrates the concordance of two stages of history, the Old Law and the New. Significantly, the texts adjacent to the two Old Testament miniatures at the side of each leaf are set out in passages of all three colours – blue, gold and red – arranged in units of three lines of each colour. At the centre, in contrast, accompanying the New Testament event which supersedes all prefigurations from the Old Law, the texts beneath the miniatures are written only in two colours – blue and gold – and in passages of two lines each. Other elements of the design that underscore binary associations around the central miniature include the subdivision of the texts of the prophet's scrolls into two differently coloured halves, the colouristic configurations of the prophet's robes, many of which are arranged in reversed, crossing patterns which play off hot red colours against cool ones, and the backgrounds of the illustrations, which contrast burnished gold for the flanking Old Testament scenes with decorated black backgrounds for the central miniatures.

Seen from these perspectives, the richly coloured script of Kings Ms 5 is more than a mere embodiment of the luxury of the manuscript. It also conveys the sacral and possibly the liturgical connotations of its subject matter and articulates its

FROM ABOVE: Fig 2, Judas receives the 30 Pieces of Silver, *flanked by Old Testament scenes,* Joseph sold by his Brothers to the Ismaelites, *and* Joseph sold by the Ismaelites to Potiphar, *British Library, London, Kings Ms 5, fol 11; Fig 4 (centre image)* Carrying of the Cross, *British Library, London, Kings Ms 5, fol 16*

42

essential binary and ternary structure. The coloured pigments of the script of Kings Ms 5 can thus be understood as aesthetic forms which express fundamental aspects of the message and meaning of the book.

The differently coloured backgrounds of the miniatures also purposefully contrast different stages of sacred history. The Old Testament events are all represented on burnished gold grounds whose brilliant and fugitive highlights hold the figures as if in suspension, constraining any tendency to view these illustrations as mere worldly narratives. In contrast, the New Testament events are all represented on architectonically designed matrices, the black and gold decoration appearing not only more active and substantial than burnished gold, but also forming a grid that anchors the figures to the picture field.

FROM ABOVE: Fig 5, Last Supper, flanked by Old Testament scenes, Abraham and Melchisedek, and Fall of Manna: Moses gives Manna to the Israelites, British Library, London, Kings Ms 5, fol 10; Fig 6 (centre image), Christ expels the Money-Changers, British Library, London, Kings Ms 5, fol 7

The Old and New Testament events are thus defined in different aesthetic terms, the burnished gold backgrounds of the former lending them a certain remote and ephemeral quality and the boldly decorated forms of the latter emphasising their greater substantiality and presence.

Although I know of no identical use of colouristically variant backgrounds to contrast different stages of sacred history, I can call attention to a later typological manuscript that displays an analogous, although different, use of colouristic distinctions to contrast events from the Old Testament with those in the New. This appears in a copy of the *Speculum Humanae Salvationis* ('Mirror of Human Salvation') written in Flanders in 1455, in which all the events from the Old Testament are depicted in grisaille, while those from the New are shown in full colour.[5] Produced approximately a half-century earlier, the 'Golden *Biblia Pauperum*' uses a different spectrum of colouristic variations in its script and the grounds of its miniatures to evoke essential distinctions between the Old and the New Testaments.

In addition to being distinctive in its formal qualities, the 'Golden *Biblia Pauperum*' is iconographically innovative. Many of the simple scenes of earlier traditions of the *Biblia Pauperum* are recast and expanded in this copy so as to elaborate their narrative and expressive content in new ways. Double narratives replace the simple, single narratives of some scenes, as in the representation of the Return of the Prodigal Son (*fig 3, rightmost image*), which depicts both the moment when the prodigal son returns to his father and a subsequent incident, when the fatted calf is killed; in earlier versions of the *Biblia Pauperum*, only the return of the son is portrayed, and without showing such evocative details as his torn clothing and the way he kneels to beg his father's forgiveness (*fig 1, lower section, rightmost image*).

'The Carrying of the Cross' in Kings Ms 5 (*fig 4*) incorporates two narrative motives found neither in the text of the *Biblia Pauperum* nor in its earlier pictorial tradition. At the left side of the miniature, St Veronica stands holding the cloth with which, according to legend, she wiped Christ's face during the ascent of Calvary and which thereupon received its miraculous imprint. The right side of the miniature portrays two men sitting in a small open house, one of them conspicuously drinking from a raised flask. This is a reference to the 'gate-watchers' and wine drinkers of Psalm 68 (69):13, which reads, 'They that sat in the gate spoke against me; and they that drank wine made me their song.' This Psalm verse is cited to characterise the purported mockery of Christ by onlookers during the Carrying of the Cross in two important Latin lives of Christ of the late Middle Ages, the *Meditationes vitae Christi* of Pseudo-Bonaventure, and Ludolph of Saxony's *Vita Christi*. As I have shown elsewhere, the imagery of this Psalm verse was most widely and fully elaborated in Dutch vernacular Passion tracts of the 15th and early-16th century.[6] The miniature in Kings Ms 5 is the earliest of a mere handful of pictorial representations of the gate-watchers and wine drinkers of the Psalm verse in a narrative representation of the Carrying of the Cross, and one of the earliest works of Northern European art to include St Veronica with her veil in this event. The motifs thus expand the anecdotal content of the miniature: situating Christ between two non-Gospel interpolations into the story of the Carrying of the Cross, they position him between one testimony to his miracle-working powers and another to the ignominy he endured from his tormentors.

Another novel way the painter of Kings Ms 5 elaborates narrative in the manuscript is to establish links across illustrations in the book. The miniature of 'Joseph sold by his brothers to the Ismaelites' (*fig 2, leftmost image*) is unusual in the first instance in showing Joseph sold to seafarers and entering their boat; usually only an exchange of money is shown, and if any reference to travel is made, it is through the presence of horses or camels. At the right side of the page (*fig 2, rightmost image*), which shows the subsequent event when Joseph is sold by the Ismaelites to Potiphar, Joseph is shown disembarking from a similar boat, thus visually suggesting that the events form a kind of continuous narrative across the page, as it were.

Some uncommon visual motifs in Kings Ms 5 establish links across one ensemble of illustrations to another. The final representation of the history of Joseph in the manuscript, which according to the accompanying text depicts Joseph making himself known to his Brothers (*fig 3, leftmost image*), shows Joseph standing on land and confronting his family in a boat. This unusual representation seems to refer back to the earlier depictions of Joseph shown sold into slavery on a boat (*fig 2*), thus effecting a new form of visual linkage among some of the Old Testament prefigurations in the manuscript.

The New Testament miniature on the same leaf, which represents Christ appearing to Mary and the Apostles (*fig 3, central image*), is unusual in showing Christ proffering large pieces of bread to the seated figures; in earlier pictorial traditions of this event, he is shown only blessing or speaking to the disciples. This uncommon iconographic motive refers to the Eucharist, as is implied by its relationship to earlier depictions in the codex. It harks back to the typological illustrations that accompany The Last Supper, where the protagonists in Abraham and Melchisedek and the Fall of Manna hold or offer similar round pieces of bread (*fig 5, left and right images*), as well as to the Last Supper itself (*fig 5, central image*), where similar round breads are displayed on the table. The effect of all these means of elaborating the narrative of individual scenes and of establishing visual links within or across individual ensembles of miniatures, is to augment the anecdotal content of the illustrations in this copy of the *Biblia Pauperum*, if not also to endow them with new historical density and resonance. Such devices accord with the new importance given to images in this manuscript, which are shown as independent, framed miniatures rather than parts of diagrammatic schemes, and enhance their capacity to draw the viewer into the life and meaning of the events they portray.

Finally, yet another way that the painter draws us into the life and meaning of his images is by showing figures and objects dramatically overlapping their frames. In the Arrest of Christ (*see page 5*), for example, Malchus and his candle are boldly portrayed as if falling out of the miniature into the lower margin. The scene of Christ expelling the Money-Changers from the Temple (*fig 6*) is even more elaborately energised: two figures are shown cut off by the frame as they flee to the left, the counting tables are depicted as if flying through the air, and coins are shown spilling over the lower frame into the margin; indeed, as if in reaction to the commotion above them, the two prophets who appear in the lower section of this page are portrayed with their backs turned to us, looking up at the event. By extending the action of these and other figures and objects in the manuscript beyond the frames that had traditionally bounded them, the miniaturist accentuates the expressive power of his illustrations and invests them with new orders of immediacy.

The 'Golden *Biblia Pauperum*' stands out as one of the most exceptional illuminated manuscripts of its day. I know of no other work that transforms so radically an existing and highly defined manuscript type, at once altering the structure of the book; its form and format; the colour scheme of its script; the layout of the page; the form and medium of its illustrations, and their iconography and expression. Kings Ms 5 fundamentally reconceives the *Biblia Pauperum*, changing its character from monastic to courtly and its illustrations from diagrams to pictures.

What is important about this manuscript is not merely that it differs in appearance from all earlier copies of the *Biblia Pauperum*. The real achievement of its artist and designer is to have altered the very way the manuscript conveys meaning, which is to say, how it structures its user's understanding and experience of its contents. The painter of the 'Golden *Biblia Pauperum*' articulates its parts and focuses and elaborates its visual interest in new ways, and in so doing he changes the protocols of reading and comprehending this kind of book. He draws the user in new ways into the function of the manuscript, into its expression, and into a new appreciation of the inner workings and implications of the relationships between the Old and New Testaments. In broader terms, the artist-designer defines and invokes new experiential dimensions of the book and its images, engaging the reader's intellect and imagination in fresh ways.

Few other medieval works of art reveal so fully how basic artistic properties – elements of pictorial structure, form, and colour – could be marshalled to reorder thoughts and experiences related to some of the most deeply held beliefs of the time. Even more than its iconography or artistic style, it is the underlying principles of design and the corollary aesthetic patterns of this book that enable it to stimulate intuited and lived experiences as well as conventionally conceptualised ones.

Notes

1 London, British Library, Kings Ms 5. For a full description and colour facsimile of the manuscript, as well as extensive discussions of such matters as the history of the *Biblia Pauperum* as a book type, the probable patrons of this copy, the historical, cultural, and artistic context in which it was created, the possible identity of the artist, related works of art, and the book's influence, see *Biblia Pauperum, Kings Ms 5, British Library, London*, 2 vols; Lucerne, Faksimile Verlag Luzern, Switzerland, 1993 (facsimile volume) and 1994 (commentary volume by Janet Backhouse, James H Marrow, and Gerhard Schmidt).

2 The standard study of the tradition is by Henrik Cornell, *Biblia Pauperum*, Stockholm, 1925, to be supplemented by Gerhard Schmidt in *Biblia Pauperum: Kings Ms 5* (see above, note 1).

3 In addition to the works cited in note 2, see Gerhard Schmidt, *Die Armenbibeln des XIV. Jahrhunderts*, Graz and Cologne, 1959.

4 Vienna, Osterreichische Nationalbibliothek, Cod Vind 1182, for which see Ernst Trenkler, *Das Evangeliar des Johann von Troppau Handschrift 1182 der osterreichischen Nationalbibliothek*, Klagenfurt and Vienna, 1948.

5 Glasgow, Hunterian Museum Library, Ms 60, for which see Adrian Wilson and Joyce Lancaster Wilson, *A Medieval Mirror: Speculum humanae salvationis 1324-1500*, Berkeley, Los Angeles and London, 1984, pp73-75, with plates.

6 James H Marrow, *Passion Iconography in Northern European Art of the Late Middle Ages and Early Renaissance: A Study of the Transformation of Sacred Metaphor into Descriptive Narrative*, Kortrijk, 1979, pp149-153.

INSERT: Fig 3, Christ appears to the Apostles, *flanked by Old Testament scenes*, Joseph makes himself known to his Brothers, *and* Return of the Prodigal Son, *in the original folded format, British Library, London, Kings Ms 5, fol 24. The reproductions in this publication are not Fine Art Facsimile quality. Figs 2-6 © Faksimile Verlag Luzern, Switzerland. The coloured insert of fig 3 of the* Biblia Pauperum, Kings Ms 3, British Library, London *was made possible by a generous subvention from the Publications Fund of the Department of Art and Archaeology at Princeton University.*

MATTER'S INSISTENCE
TONY SCHERMAN'S *BANQUO'S FUNERAL*
Andrew Benjamin

The funeral of Banquo, murdered by Macbeth, is an occurence that will have to have taken place even though it does not feature in Shakespeare's play. And yet positing the necessity of an event that cannot be situated in that from which it arises complicates the hold of fiction by demanding that it generate its own fiction; a fiction giving a different sense of reality to the place of generation. Such must be the case with Banquo's funeral. What type of occurrence would it be? While this question may have general applicability, in this instance it is quite precise; a series of paintings portray elements surrounding the funeral. Consequently with any questioning of the nature of this occurrence the problematic presence of representation will be central to it. Moreover, what compounds the problem is the recognition that these paintings are ostensibly figurative and hence already implicated in representation. However, can they be taken to narrate Banquo's funeral? At this stage there is a need for caution in so far as these works – Tony Scherman's group of paintings entitled *Banquo's Funeral* – are partial since they only show elements of the subject matter[1] (and yet is an element always part of a whole?). As a beginning, however, it is perhaps expedient to start with the more general question; how do figurative paintings narrate? While this latter question will need to be pursued, it harbours the possibility that cojoining the terms narrative and painting will be to have made a type of category mistake. Why is it that paintings should be thought to narrate?

What marks out the work of narrative is time. To follow a narrative is to allow for the sequential continuity within which it unfolds. Narrative does not repeat the work of chronological time but allows it to be presented and thus allows events to be acted out. Within any narrative, what becomes important is not the relationship to chronology but the relationship to sequence; even the use of an interrupted sequence or the presentation of disrupted moments still unfold sequentially. Narrative becomes the way of tracing the determining effect of time within the self-realisation of literature and film. The relationship between time and that which is narrated has neither a generalisable nor an ideal form. In broad terms, the nature of the relationship between time and the narrated – and here the contrast will need to be as great as that between, for example, Virginia Woolf's *The Waves* and Zola's *La fortune des Rougon* – would become a

way of identifying the presence of one generic form or style rather than another. While it is possible to provide a structural description of a literary work, part of what marks out the process of reading is the place of time; not just the time of reading, but the way what is read is temporalised. The relationship between reading and narrative is only explicable in terms of a series of complex temporal relationships.

With a painting, the nature of the relationship between the viewer and the viewed is going to be obviously, though nonetheless importantly, different. Paintings are not read. The self-realisation of the novel – a realisation that in every sense of the term comes to be read – is not present within painting. Paintings are temporalised differently. This point can be pursued by examining the narrative force of Poussin's *The Nurture of Jupiter*. In order to save the infant Jupiter from the fate of his siblings he was taken to Crete and raised by two nymphs. For food he had milk and honey. Poussin's painting shows the infant suckling, and one of the nymphs gathering honey; furthermore he is positioned – abandoned in the act of nourishing himself – under the calm and secure gaze of a shepherd and another nymph. Safety is reinforced by the way in which the suckling infant is placed in relation to his guardians. While they are attentive, he is only attending to himself. Nor only is the serenity of the location – Mount Ida – staged by the work's own internal ordering, there is also the order and calm benevolence of the setting in which the infant Jupiter is present. While it is possible to provide a more elaborate description of the painting, the question that must be taken up concerns what can be provisionally described as its narrative content.

The painting provides a moment from the story of Jupiter's survival. The story is not complete. Hesiod is needed in order that the detail and consequence of that survival be known. Here, there is a moment, a part. And yet even an element of a longer and more detailed narrative may still have narrative content. What may be missing, however, is the narrative time appropriate to literature and film. The reality and practicality of Jupiter's survival are demonstrated. The fruits of Rhea's cunning can be seen. And yet describing what is seen, even locating it within the myth's larger frame necessitates effacing – to a greater or lesser degree – the work's material presence. Materiality is not the simple reduction of the work to that which

Nicolas Poussin, The Nurture of Jupiter, *oil on canvas, 96.2 x 119.6cm*

has a painted presence. Paint's presence can be held apart from materiality in so far as the former is straightforwardly concerned with the way in which content is ordered and presented; in other words, it is explicable in terms of how time figures within a work whose own work is determined by the presence of figures. In contrast, materiality can be understood within painting as the insistence of the medium within the generation of the work's meaning. With ostensibly figurative painting, what becomes of interest are the possible points of overlap between paint's presence and materiality. The effect of allowing for a contingent rather than necessary connection between these two determinations is that it will allow for a reworking of the figurative. The figurative will no longer be reducible to the mere presence of figures within the frame.

The shepherd and the nymph hold the goat while Jupiter suckles. They do not need to keep watch. Jupiter is safe from external threat. Spatial positioning narrates the emotional and psychological dimension of the work. That positioning is given to the viewer. The detail of what is given comes to be reinforced, while simultaneously emerging as more nuanced and subtle, as the work is viewed. The capacity for more to emerge is not just a claim about the work's detail, it has to do with the continuity of the work being given. Painting will in general eschew the possibility of 'at-onceness' precisely because of the way it is present.[2] And yet the contrast should not be taken as between a type of simultaneity on the one hand, and the process of sequential continuity on the other. Words have, after all, a type of immediacy. The frame does not order time in terms of sequence. It is rather that establishing the relations between moments within the frame involves a process of seeing that is neither continuous nor discontinuous. What takes place is the gradual emergence of a network of viewed relations which allow for the attribution to the work of a certain narrative quality. Any attempt to describe what is taking place becomes a description of the elements of narration rather than of the process of narrating. This process is almost exclusively confined to the relationship between the viewer and the viewed. It is as though the temporality of the narrative of literature or film was necessarily absent. Accounting for that absence necessitates recourse to time. The medium is necessarily different but each medium has its own temporality. Time will plot the real differences.

Paint's presence is already a complex interplay of spatial determinations and temporal considerations. In sum, with this form of presence space – though more exactly spacing – will itself have already acquired an inherent temporality that cannot be eliminated. Taking up these considerations demands the introduction of a further element.

It is not just that Poussin's *The Nurture of Jupiter* is a painting, it is constrained to work as a painting. Evidence of that constraint is clear from its necessary differentiation from film and literature. Time does not unfold sequentially within a painting. And yet the question that returns concerns the work's own relation to the operation of painting. How is it that this work works as painting? There are two elements involved in answering this question. They will need to draw upon the distinction between paint's presence and materiality. Indeed, in terms of that distinction it will become possible to reintroduce the concerns and thus the interpretive demands of Tony Scherman's *Banquo's Funeral*; a site that is already demanding since it is already located off centre. The first point touches on what has already been raised concerning time; the temporality that determines paint's presence. While the second introduces the complex problem of the nature of 'what' it is that is present. Here the question of the 'what' cannot be answered by recourse to a simple description unless the description brings with it the determining effect of time; time within painting. As has already been suggested the depiction of the scene is a depiction of a moment. The moment in question, however, will differ significantly from a film still in so far as the still has been excised from a medium of which it is a part. For the still to be analysed cinematically, it would need to be returned to the film of which it forms a constitutive part. Here, the painting – while a moment – is not part of a whole which has the same medium. To that extent, the painting brings with it a type of interiority; an interiority that will differ with different types of painting. This interiority is already subjected, therefore, to the differing temporalities that will mark out paint's presence. While the more exacting problem is the extent to which this presence and the temporality in question are mediated by the work's material presence, it remains the case that here, interiority will always be traversed or worked on by external elements. Interiority will never be sustained absolutely.

In the case of Poussin's painting, its material presence works to effect the staged order. Paint work provides no more than the intricate positioning of bodies that are themselves – in the productive nature of their staged relation – the construction of security and safety. Paint's work does not intrude into the construction and realisation of this order. Moreover, once there is the staging of order then there is both a position from which it is to be viewed and thus a surface that while resisting the possibility of a simple giving, since it will allow for the depth of time demanded by paint's presence, nonetheless forms itself into a self-defined moment. What is provided is a type of *nunc stans* – though now one with depth – to be viewed. While this is a position integral to Poussin's own aesthetic, what it marks out is the necessary distancing of materiality.[3] The importance of recognising this limit is not to construct a series of restrictive limits for Poussin, but to allow for a development within painting in which paint's presence will come to be mediated by materiality. With this mediation, as shall be argued, meaning or representation will give way to a more pronounced sense of work and signification. While the propriety of painting is maintained by the attribution of paint's presence, what is proper to painting will have opened up once the intrusion of materiality is taken into consideration.

While this argument repeats those themes within the development of modernist aesthetics that focused upon the centrality of the medium, this identification was usually equated with either a generic form – one in which the actual determination of the genre went unexamined – or the presence of the medium was conflated with the presence of its effect. An example of this last point would be the claim that the work of paint generated a surface that could be experienced in its totality at one time. After all, this is the basis of Greenberg's interpretation of Abstract Expressionism. Holding to this position works to create a surface whose projection, because it was thought to be simultaneous with its being experienced, would in some sense also be timeless. Not only would this efface the effect of paint's presence, it would in addition preclude the possibility of any integration of materiality into the work's work. What will need to be allowed for is the productive presence of time and the work of the medium that precludes the twofold reduction to genre or unified object that otherwise would have been given by the inter-articulation of paint's presence and materiality. As has already been intimated, the affirmation of their relation will preclude the absolute, and thus all encompassing, hold of generic divisions and in so doing allow for openings in which both the genre and, in this instance, the activity of painting are able to be given within an inaugurating repetition. In being reworked, the genre will be retained.

Weaving the thread of narrative back through these concerns – remembering that in part the question to be addressed was how appropriate the term narrative might in fact be in regards to painting – is best undertaken in relation to Scherman's actual paintings. As a group, what marks these works out is the staged relation to an occurrence within a play that is itself not staged within the play. However, rather than presenting this other moment within the same conventions – ie, another play staging that which was not itself staged within the original play – here there is a shift to painting.[4] Already, the work of painting has been singled out. Despite its having been identified in this way, the mere location of painting cannot form the basis of any attribution to these works of an insistent singularity. The singular will need to be sought elsewhere; not by deferring painting but by making the question of painting far more precise. As a beginning, addressing the singular will need to take place in terms of narrative.

It is already clear that what has been identified thus far as paint's presence will begin to account for the specific content of particular paintings. For example, with regard to the presentation of Lady Macbeth in *Banquo's Funeral: Lady Macbeth*, the shoe – the high heeled shoe on a leg crossed over another, the shoe of the latter muted by the work's own inscription on to the canvas – introduces a staged nonchalance bringing with it its own provocation; a created mood jarring with the intended solemnity of the title. Already the picture of Lady Macbeth is cast. Inscribed within the work is a staging of the relationship between death and sexuality that necessitates a metonymic connection between the shoe and Lady Macbeth herself. She is eroticised. The shoe, in terms of its determining the space of a type of fetishism, in addition to its seemingly inappropriate place within the solemnity of the rituals accompanying death, works to eroticise the name Lady Macbeth. Furthermore the eroticisation of the site demands, because of the specificity of the relationship between sexuality and death, another possibility for that complex relation. Here, paint's presence creates a site that is already overdetermined. Part of what sanctions this description is the inability of that which is present within the frame to hold and control the scene that has been created. It is not a question either of figure or representation, were they to be taken as ends in themselves: what is presented can be described. However, how does what is described, or has been described, work within the overall work? Once this question is asked of a painting that operates almost exclusively on the level of paint's presence, then the answer is already constrained by the nature of the relationship between work and the specificity of what has been described. In the case of the Poussin painting cited above, the relationship could be characterised in terms of an approximating coextensivity. What necessitates the qualification of 'approximating' is the temporality proper to paint's work. It is the sheer impossibility of the simultaneity of giving and receiving that demands the introduction of this restriction. While this restriction is fundamental, in order for the painting's own work to be presented accurately, the significant correlation to this approximation is the elimination of materiality. In other words, part of this coextensivity is the

elimination of the inscribed presence of the work's production from forming an integral part of the way it works. Once there is the centrality of the paint's presence, then the meaning of the work becomes the relationship between the elements that have been presented; remembering that this presentation takes place in terms of the temporality of painting's presence. In the case of the emerging centrality of materiality – the continual effectuation of the work as work – it will still be the case that paint's presence forms an indelible part of the way the object is to be attributed meaning. However, rather than establishing a semantic range incorporating a variety of meanings, meaning will be allowed to yield its place to signification once materiality takes over from the domination of painting's presence.[5] Clearly, one of the consequences of this position is that the hold of the genre of the figurative – or of representation within painting – in becoming reworked, marks out the presence of an already inscribed complexity. In other words, rather than assuming that the specificity of the given is already established, the identity of the given will become the site in which what endures as a question is the determination of the genre. A fixed identity gives way to the incorporation of a conception of identity as the continuity of the question of identity. More will be in play with the figure than the mere presence of figures. It is with Tony Scherman's paintings – with their particularity – that there is another opening; a different form of being present. Here, what defines the alterity in question is the emergent dominance of materiality. At the outset what characterises the difference has already been mentioned. The hold of the framed is no longer absolute. And yet this should not be understood as the claim that the frame, in presenting only part of the body, gestures to an outside that has not been contained. Indeed, the necessity to describe the relationship between the foot and Lady Macbeth as metonymic is intended to indicate that her presence has been inscribed within the whole. Moreover, part of what determines her inscription – that which gives it its actual quality – is the eroticisation stemming from the presence of the shoe. Prior to taking up the material detail of this painting, it is important to situate it in relation to a number of others which in the first place provides details of Lady Macbeth's face, and in the second purport to present the witches.

The works presenting Lady Macbeth show incomplete faces. In one instance the face is incomplete because it is literally a detail and in another its being incomplete stems from the way in which the actual production of the work allows the face to emerge. In this latter instance, what is remarkable is that what is present does not emerge from a background. It is as though the face is crafted. Two issues occur that will have to be taken up. The first can be described as the disruption of the figure/ground relation, while the second arises from the necessity of having to clarify the description of the face as crafted. In a sense, however, these two points will intersect. The disruption of the figure/ground relation is effected by the way the faces

Banquo's Funeral, 'Lady Macbeth', *1995, encaustic on canvas, 152 x 152cm*

are present. Their presence is explicable not in terms of the sheer presentation of a face, but from the way they are held by the work's matter, which is such that the face begins to work its way out of the matter. The faces arise, but not from a ground. They occur within the work. Whatever force this emergence has, it has it in relation to the traditional presence of the attribution of the figure/ground relation. After all, this relationship has been taken to permeate all genres of painting. As such it can be viewed as the traditional method by which spatial presence is introduced into the work of painting; even though it may be an introduction given by the act of interpretation.

The figure/ground relation would characterise painting to the extent that depiction was thought in terms of either representation of the mere presentation of figures. Even in the case of paint's presence, there is the introduction of an economy – a timing of space and the spacing of time – that defers the possible introduction of the figure/ground relation. Again, insisting on this economy is to insist on the propriety of painting. The difference occurs here because of the centrality or resistance to representation. (In sum the figure/ground relation is only thinkable in terms of the centrality of representation. The figures provide the representation and the ground is paint's provision of its condition of possibility.) Moreover, with the introduction of materiality, another element will come to inform the frame. In this instance, non-acceptance of the twofold distinction in which the figure is given in relation to an already given ground arises because the work of matter will have transformed that relation. However, the transformation will not be simply an interpretive act that repositions the opposition. It is rather that the work's own work imposes itself. What insists is a particular type of work. The specific use of encaustic produces a framed presence that no longer enables an easy distinction to be drawn between the setting and that which is set within it. What is at work within these paintings is another possibility. It is not just that on one level there is an overall surface that seems to contain the work; a surface refusing differentiation because this is the wax's effect.

There is, in addition, a disruption of the surface, as an effect of the surface. It occurs because the nature of what has been applied, encaustic, breaks the surface and in so doing causes both head and surround – and there is not simply a head and its given surround but rather there is both head and surround given within and as painting – to show a copresence; an incorporation into the process of painting, that positions both elements to be worked and to work equally. Their copresence breaks the traditional interdependency and, moreover, the possibility of any staged relation. The relation could not be reintroduced. There is, therefore, neither figure nor ground. What is occurring demands a different description. Responding to this demand means accepting the constraint of the work's material presence. Matter causes the disruption of the traditional categories of interpretation. Matter insists. In the specific instance

of the two paintings of Lady Macbeth (see opposite and back cover) not only is there the fraying of the hold of portraiture – even of a fictional portrait – by the presence of faces that are not the same, the difference can be taken as portraying a particular conception both of subjectivity and the subject Lady Macbeth. Her disseminated presence in these works is both her presence at the funeral – it should not be forgotten that the series of paintings has the general title *Banquo's Funeral* – an event staged outside the fictional site, as well as her charged and complex presence within the play.

With these paintings there is neither just the head of a woman, nor is there the attempt to represent the interplay of ambition and power. The heads, once understood as the work of painting, entail that the staged presence within theatre has not been given another theatrical setting. In the move to painting, the question of her identity and thus her motives become linked to her mode of being present. Any attempt to provide further detail of the actual heads becomes the attempt to describe paint's work. What is meant by crafted, therefore, is the creation of the head as within and as part of the work. It neither presents nor represents a character for the precise reason that the space of representation is no longer productively present within frame. In addition, rather than viewing the heads as either there in part or as incomplete – as though both these states of affairs gestured towards a set up in which completion was to be enacted *tout court* – completion turns into a dissembling presence. In the first place, it would gesture towards the subject position construed as present to self and secondly, it would have to efface the way materiality is at work within these paintings. The crafted presence of the head is the affirmation of matter, and as part of that affirmation matter's presence signifies by holding a presentation of the face that is never one.

While it is tempting to situate the presence of the witches only in relation to the role they have within the play – particularly in regard to their prophetic quality – in this instance such an opening would merely contextualise the characters but with the consequence of denying the specificity of painting. What is involved here is the painted presence of that which must be defined in relation to Macbeth, but as painting's work. The extraordinary moment in the play – Act IV Scene 1, in which Macbeth encounters the witches, Hecate, the different Apparitions and Banquo's ghost – introduces within the structure of the theatrical development a moment that seems to elude the possibility of naming but not of theatrical presentation. When, on encountering the witches, Macbeth asks what they are doing, he receives the reply, 'A deed without a name'. Macbeth then appeals to their prophetic powers. What is left to one side is the 'deed'. The direct referent is the cauldron and the creation of magic. The activity was seen by the audience, though not necessarily by Macbeth. The witches cannot name the 'deed'. Here, a certain theatrical convention is maintained. Preparation and transformation are enacted through time; not only the transformation of the cauldron's contents, but equally the Apparitions. Here, mystery is created by the procession of Apparitions. The magical effect of the witches is reinforced by the predictions that will have taken on the form of riddles by the play's end. The question for painting concerns the possibility of a 'deed without a name'.

Within theatre, the deed the witches refused to name was still present. It still had been experienced and the impossibility of naming – though equally the refusal to name – neither restricted presence nor experience. Indeed, the theatrical effect was heightened by holding to the lack of necessity. The activity with the cauldron maintained its evocative power – a power mediating what takes place throughout the rest of the scene and on into the play – precisely because it is not named. Theatre allows for a temporality in which the power of a refusal, or the force of an unspoken gesture will continue to mediate and to recast earlier occurrences. The transformation of the witches in Scherman's painting cannot be understood in the same way. While theatre can use its own resources, these resources are absent from the way the contents of a painting are staged. What then does it mean to paint a witch? How is their presence made precise within painting as painting?

Scherman uses two different approaches to the Witches. If no one else was, they must have been at *Banquo's funeral*. The question is, how would they have been present? What form would their presence have taken? All of these questions concerning either the presence of witches or the way they are made present address a similar issue once painting – the activity of painting – is taken as central. After all, once theatrical conventions are left to one side, one of the problems that endures is recognising the witch. With the series of paintings *Banquo's Funeral,* a problem arises for this very reason. On one level the paintings of Lady Macbeth cannot be readily distinguished from the paintings of the Witches. There is, however, a painting of Hecate in the form of a stag. The stag, as with all of the figures in this series, emerges as if from the painting; not from the background but from the paint itself. It is transformed by a movement in which a stag starts to become and then is present. The figure's identity therefore has to be, though as the process of becoming-present. It is thus that there is no ground; no stage on which it appears. It is in its appearing. Paint works by staging that appearance. The work's work is the appearance's becoming-present. Appearance will be the work's truth content in so far as appearance is materiality. Here, matter's insistence is the work' presence. In sum, it is precisely because the stag does enter from out of the mist, or from the fog, and yet it is entering, coming to presence, that paint will have been at work in a significantly different way. While this description of the work *Hecate as Stag* addresses certain elements of the work, what has yet to be taken up is the transformation of Hecate; Hecate as stag. It is with the question of this transformation, coupled to the problem of distinguishing

between the Witches and Lady Macbeth, that it will be possible to return to the problem of the relationship between narrative and painting and thus to conclude. Here, however, concluding will mean plotting the limit of Scherman's own work. It should be added, of course, that it is inevitable that, at some point, all work will encounter its own limit.

The difficulty that occurs concerns the problematic relationship between materiality and narrative. Another way of formulating the issue is whether or not a distinction can be drawn between Lady Macbeth and the Witches – a distinction other than one given by the title – in terms of materiality? Or does the distinction depend upon the reintroduction of content other than matter in order to establish and thus hold the distinction in place? Equally, the problem with *Hecate as Stag* is the extent to which this transformation and thus the magical nature of the act could be given content by the work's material presence? Or does such a transformation necessitate the incorporation of an outside in order to determine the work's meaning? The extent to which this latter possibility becomes real is the extent to which materiality would come to be effaced. The force of these questions derives from the fact that they arise out of a consideration of the work's effective presence. They occur, in other words, as part of a response to the work's work.

These questions hinge on narrative. Poussin's *The Nurture of Jupiter* can be given a narrative quality since independently of the work's material presence – its presence as a painting, as painting's work – it stages an occurrence. What occurs is what paint's presence provides. Describing it, utilising the resources of mythology, become ways of attributing a meaning to the work. Part of the process of attribution will involve the meaning or interpretation of the myth itself and then the subsequent attempt to trace the connection between the already existent narrative and the actual formulation or presentation of an element of the myth within the work. While at no stage wishing to diminish the effect of the work as proper to painting, it can still be argued that the question of its meaning cannot be given in relation to the work as pure interiority. Only by allowing for a relationship between the exterior and the interior does It become possible to detail what is occurring. This is the case not because the painting is figurative, nor because it is the representation of a particular moment within the more general mythological story, but because the work of paint – materiality – does not intrude into the work such that it contributes to the generation of the work's meaning. Painting's presence entails that the work's meaning is maintained because of painting but as indifferent to its material presence.

In contrast to the work of paint's presence within Poussin, Scherman's paintings can initially be viewed as opening up the space of materiality. With regard to the paintings of Lady Macbeth's shoes, the crossed legs, the relationship between the legs, the contrast of shoes, the presence of one and the dissipation of the other and thus the insistent quality of the presented shoe, are staged by the operation of the medium. It is there in the work's work. This ordering needs to incorporate the presence of the shoe and thus the effective eroticisation of the site that the shoe sets in motion. Nonetheless, the extent to which it is at work is because of the operation of the medium: it is sustained by materiality. It is thus that the work signifies. The problem that inheres in Scherman's work, however, is the possibility of it having to depend upon a relationship between exteriority and interiority in order to account for the work's own effectuation. It can be described as a problem due to the fact that once this relation becomes dominant in accounting for the operation of the work's work then this occurs at the expense of materiality.

With regard to the painting *Hecate as Stag,* the interpretive difficulty concerns having to account for Hecate's transformation within the framework of materiality. Even though it may involve exaggerating the significance of the title, the central problem is accounting for the 'as' – *Hecate as Stag* – that sets the context for the work. Can this transformation occur within the work's work? The painting itself presents the stag such that, as has been suggested, its presence is set by the way in which it presents itself within the work. Its being there is to be accounted for in terms of materiality. While a figure – perhaps in the most trivial sense also a representation – its figuring is a direct result of the way in which the medium allows for its presence. Thus far, the work maintains its materiality. However, once it is also claimed that the stag is Hecate as a stag, such a transformation be may be allowed in mythological or literary terms but not a transformation effected by the work's work. It has been brought about for it, prior to it and therefore exterior

to it. Therefore, the force of the 'as' remains indifferent to the painting's material presence. This point can, of course, be extended to account for the problem of differentiating between Lady Macbeth and the Witches. In sum, what is involved is the refusal to allow painting to set the measure of its own work.

Reformulating this position in terms of narrative, results in the necessity for painting to retain its position as painting; ie, holding to painting's mode of narration. In the case of Poussin this occurs because of paint's presence, and yet at the same time depends upon a narrative form that is dissimilar to painting. While Poussin's *The Nurture of Jupiter* inscribed a complex temporality within it, in part because it remained indifferent to materiality, Scherman's *Hecate as Stag* is absolutely attentive to materiality and thus eschews what has been described as paint's presence, even though the project of the painting – the presence of Hecate as a stag – would be better executed in terms of paint's presence than it would in terms of materiality. Materiality becomes an almost unnecessary element despite the fact that its power as a painting – the sedulous hold exercised over the viewer – is derived almost completely from its materiality and not from its being the appearance of Hecate as a stag. Signification failed to provide Hecate as a stag. The transformation was only present on the level of meaning. It is precisely the presence of this limit within Scherman's work – a limit that divides the work as well as traversing it – that attests to its importance. The response made by his paintings to the question of the relationship between narrative and painting works to define with greater precision the contours of that relationship, even though part of his work is unable to work within them. It is the limit, after all, that yields painting's insistence.

Notes

1 I will refer to these works as paintings, and in addition refer to what will be developed as paint's work, throughout this paper. The material used in their creation is 'encaustic on canvas'. Paint's work need not refer to paint as such, but rather it designates ways in which the work's material presence intrudes into the object. As will be suggested, this intrusion opens up the space of signification.

2 I have developed a critique of Greenberg's formulation of 'at-onceness' in *What is Abstraction?,* Academy Editions, London, 1996. In sum, what is involved is a distinction between an ontological or temporal simplicity, a simplicity that in the end is putative, and a form of complexity. This conception of complexity has been treated in Andrew Benjamin, *The Plural Event,* Routledge, London, 1993.

3 The detail of this position could be pursued via a close reading of the report of Poussin's letter to de Noyes, 1642. What would need to be studied is the relationship between 'eye' and 'object' developed as

part of what Poussin identifies as 'le Prospect'. See *Correspondance de Nicolas Poussin,* Archives de l'Art Français, Nouvelle Période, Tome V, 1968, pp139-47.

4 The most celebrated example of this convention within theatre would be Tom Stoppard's *Rosencrantz and Guildenstern are Dead.*

5 All that can be done here is sketch the nature of the distinction between meaning and signification. Meaning is, in sum, the hold over the object of elements that are generically exterior to it but which play a fundamental role in its being understood. Signification, on the other hand, allows for allusion to an exterior but only to the extent that the allusion does not restrict the centrality of materiality and thus materiality being the basis of any understanding of the object. Meaning and signification are not to be taken as an absolute either/or. Nonetheless, they frame different activities within painting.

ARCHITECTURE OF THE MIND
MACHINE INTELLIGENCE AND ABSTRACT PAINTING
David Moos

*I suspect that all really higher intelligences will be machines.
Unless they're beyond machines. But biological intelligence
is a lower form of intelligence, almost inevitably. We're in
an early stage in the evolution of intelligence but at a late
stage in the evolution of life. Real intelligence won't be
living.*[1] (Arthur C Clarke, 1970)

Context proffers the guise within which the antithetical may
masquerade. Consider a work of architecture. If seen along
the skyline, from a distance the building blends in. Close up,
however, its otherness is revealed: a windowless structure
over 40 storeys high. The surface is comprised of tiled together
granite slabs, each a discrete unit within the overall complexion.
Natural alterations in the tone of the granite provide articulation
within the otherwise completely integrated edifice that posits
itself as monolithic object. Reaching skyward in bound columnar
sections, the building is crowned by a series of vents. These
ducts are screened with metallic black slats, shielding view
into or through the structure.

At ground level this challenge of access is reiterated. Along
one side there is a ramp leading, below street level, to a
sealed-off garage. The building possesses no plaza or clear
lobby, offering only stairs that lead to diminutive glass doors.
Thus, the experience at ground level is synonymous with the
skyline view: the building has no orientation and discloses
nothing about its function.

The only visible intercourse with the environment is supplied
by the vents, through which air presumably passes. The building
would seem to breathe, exchange outside atmosphere, and
thus operate a metaphor of communication. To learn that this
is the AT&T Long Lines Building transfigures both its form and
content. It is a machine, a vast switch-board, standing as
totem at the dawn of a new organisational age that has become
our computer-assisted global urban environment. Completed
in 1974, the AT&T Long Lines Building is a so-called 'equipment
building'[2] in which the telephone company houses the hardware
and software of telecommunications. Without it the present-
day city would functionally cease to exist. 'It would be difficult
to visualize the rise of skylines, the agglomeration of skyscrapers,'
geographer and urban theroist Jean Gottman suggests, 'without
the telephone smoothing out the functioning of such a complex

and integrated system'.[3] If indeed the city is a system, then the
Long Lines Building is that vital fabricated component
responsible for the structuring of all urban communications
not conducted physically face-to-face, in person. This is the
skyscraper upon which the operation of all others depends. In
the presence of this building any connotations of the human
linked to corporeality vanish.

As architecture the Long Lines Building, built by John Carl
Warnecke & Associates, attracts little attention, in contrast to
Philip Johnson's AT&T Tower of one decade later, a building
that singles itself out as corporate herald of postmodernity.

These observations relate the Long Lines Building to
conditions of its visual experience – an encounter that reveals
little about its internal functioning. Given this opacity, one
option for the pursuit of meaning would be to follow Charles
Jencks' proposal that 'analogy' operates as skeleton key to
decoding the syntax of a new architecture: 'People invariably
see one building in terms of another, or in terms of a similar
object; in short, as a metaphor. The more unfamiliar a Modern
building is, the more they will compare it metaphorically to
what they know.'[4]

To approach the Long Lines Building with 'analogy' would,
however, simply service expectation. To regard the building
as a 'metaphor', and classify it as one among the plethora of
tall buildings, would undervalue if not entirely misapprehend
its radical nature. The building is a machine – a supercomputer
posing in the form of skyscraper. Thus, the status of this object
denies belonging to any lineage enabling narration within an
architectural continuum, Modern or Post-Modern.

This structure presses architecture to its limits. The Modernist
dialectical pair of form/function ceases to pertain. Form becomes
negligible, emerging as automatic consequence of function.
The Long Lines Building articulates impenetrability, subserving
the very essence of what telecommunication *is*. The building
is not simply an embodiment of information, but is information
fulfilling its *own* processes exclusively for itself as a constructed
manifestation. It maintains a consummate form: impregnable,
autonomous, in command of its being and governed by its
own necessities. As machinic sheath, a hardware organism, it
has organised its substance to embody the agency of what
Gottmann has called 'fungible space'.[5] An object full of mobile

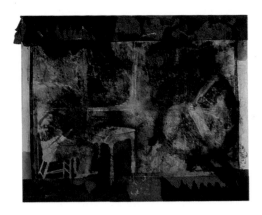

data, pulsing information: all location – the places of sender/ receiver – must pass through the Long Lines Building. The tropes of speed, transmission, and circulation are possible only through the entelechy of this machine.

As an object it maintains material embodiment, yet as a working machine it presents the condition of unpicturability. Information has no image; the messages coiling through the Long Lines Building in coded sequences have no fixed appearance. 'More than any other machine the computer is principally a *concept*', one theorist observes 'The computer becomes whatever machine it controls'.[6] In this case, it assumes the incidental form of a skyscraper; the machines it mediates are the extensions of man.

In a 1983 painting entitled *The Computer Moves In*, Sigmar Polke portrayed the relationship between man and computer. Painting is seen to move between two characteristic vocabularies, the figurative and the abstract, conflating each in an effort to depict the regime of information exchange. Blindfolded and strapped to a chair, the human subject sits before a desk-top computer, confronting the eruptive experience of data-reflux. The terrain modelled by the machine – everything about the painting that is not the human figure – connotes an energised volatility that threatens to overwhelm, implode into the central vortex of white light. An amorphous storm of information, painting is seen to reach its embattled limits.

Designation of 'the computer' in *The Computer Moves In* requires the replete repertoire of the painting: its pre-printed, polka-dotted fabric support, sewn together yet flagging over the top-left edge; a host of techniques that co-opt the virtuous glyphs of Abstract Expressionism, as well as stain or Colour-Field saturation methods; and, also, the silhouetting language of figuration. Through the commingling of painting's established codes, Polke configures a prescient pictorial commentary about man's relation to the computer. Ominous as this image may seem, it is a painting, and like all painting, relies upon the artist's body to formulate its being. Beyond the prone, captive of the machine shown within the picture, the body of the artist masquerades to perform the task of painting itself.

This paradigmatic image sets up the demands for painting in the age of artificial intelligence. In response to the computer, painting escalates its means to the limits of syntactic malleability.

Shuttling across a vast domain of gesture, Polke summons an array of mark-making, from the prudent mimetic touch to turbulent swings of the body in motion. His method narrates the escape painting may provide from the incursion of the machine.

Elaborating such a polarised position between culture and technology is not, however, the aim of this essay, but rather to analyse and understand how painting can vitally inform and even infuse developments transpiring within the discipline of Artificial Intelligence. As artifacts of human consciousness, both material and image based, painting may be considered to contain coded networks of activity which have proven elusive to the computational acuity.

Pronouncements currently emanating from the Artificial Intelligence community speak with a rationale ('we have not the slightest grounds for believing that human brains are not machines'[7]), that would seem to make intercourse with cultural criticism an unwieldy endeavour. Who for instance speaks of the brain when experiencing an abstract painting? Yet if the project of AI (as it is referred to) appears predominantly scientific and at times ominous, closer scrutiny reveals that it is deeply concerned with creativity and abstraction. These tropes of human consciousness, typified by abstract painting, can be considered the preeminent battle grounds where crucial debates in AI rage. After initial successes with physical mastery, especially in the fields of automation and robotics, AI has become increasingly preoccupied with the philosophical precincts of the human organism. To build a truly intelligent machine, the ambition declares, necessitates inclusion of those properties designating the human as the highest-order organism: the architecture of the system should mimic with an infinite degree of accuracy the architecture of the mind.[8]

One pitfall with this objective is that it conceives the project along a representational plane. In fact, the thinking that underlies this approach implicitly presumes human intelligence the sole and supreme ledger of elaboration – that like God (the narrative goes) we are only able to create in our own image. Hubris in believing that we are unique to the universe, it would seem more productive to postulate an Artificial Intelligence as eventually constituting a valid *Other Intelligence*. The perspective for developing this alterity is one given by abstract painting, which comes into contact, or more properly inter-

AT&T Long Lines Building, *John Carl Warnecke & Associates, 1974 (photos, Julie Trempe). The AT&T Long Lines Center was designed to house telecommunications equipment and to protect it and the building's personnel in the event of atomic attack. The four-storey-high 'archer's gallery' at the roof shields the giant long-line microwave horns which beam messages to relay stations 48.3km away and up to hanging satellites positioned high above the city. The radiation-resistant, windowless fortress maintains the capacity to protect a population of 1,500 operating personnel within the building for two weeks if necessary.*

venes, with the central strategies underpinning the enterprise of Artificial Intelligence.

The form and contents of an Other may be difficult to discern. As the Long Lines Building indicates, external facades inhere as diversionary codings of content. In Bernard Tschumi's view: 'There is no longer a causal relationship between buildings and their content, their use, and, their very improbable meaning'.[9] Vision alone will fail to describe buildings' 'meaning'. Such a paradigm, prompted through the implementation of telematic technologies, if transcribed to painting would provoke a paradoxical position, where vision requires assistance from other faculties. This would fracture the transparent relationship between painting and opticality. The merger of surface, form and contents that painting supposes must then be bracketed and displaced to other registers of cognition.

Probing for the Other demands apprehension of where motives and mandate loosen from perception. Thus, in this essay, the seductions of cyberspace are left behind. The norm for cultural criticism until now has been to engage new computer-related technologies along a trajectory of the products that have been created.[10] Here, however, we are not interested in the kinds of images or experiences of images that new technologies generate for culture, but rather investigate how Artificial Intelligence formulates its own developmental problematics *for itself*.

What would it mean to think and to perceive digitally? A more radical model than Jencks' proposal of 'Analogy' is required as his prescription for attributing meaning, in keeping with postmodern theory, emerges as inadequate here (the more 'unfamiliar' a manifestation is, the more one begins to compare it to what one knows). Suppose our knowledge of the present does not equip our acculturated minds to 'metaphorically' ingest the scope of Artificial Intelligence?

The required paradigm shift begins with the basic plan of understanding that machine intelligence necessarily adopts and thus demands a divergent conceptual strategy. Cognitive psychologist Margaret Boden has pointed out that

... most computers are *digital* systems, in which the basic units either 'fire' or they don't. The brain, on the other hand, is to a large extent an *analogue* device: synaptic activity varies continuously (and nerve cells often fire 'spontaneously' as a result). Digital computers are designed as *serial* devices, in which only one instruction is executed at a time. By contrast, the brain is a parallel-processing device: neurones have rich interconnections, which enable cells to encourage or inhibit their neighbors' activity.[11]

The human brain is a quite different mechanism to a digital computer, if one differentiates these 'devices' at a structural level. The search for 'rich interconnections' that may transpire 'spontaneously' is a process that eludes machine intelligence. The question remains as to whether this cerebral process, natural to the human mind, should be imposed upon machines as a core necessity.

Resisting the temptation to humanise the machine, Paul Virilio proposes a divergent performative criteria. He is right in his appraisal of the impact that artificial vision will have upon our entire method of relating to and relaying the world through our faculty of sight. In *The Vision Machine*, Virilio describes a fabricated 'perceptron', an 'absolute-speed machine' that would undermine traditional notions of geometrical optics such as observables and non-observables:

> Don't forget that 'image' is just an empty word here since the machine's interpretation has nothing to do with normal vision. For the computer, the optically active electron image is merely a series of coded impulses whose configuration we cannot begin to imagine since, in this 'automation of perception', *image feedback is no longer assured*.[12]

In a world advanced beyond sight how should one begin to theorise subjectivity; how should we place ourselves in relation to ourselves? Such a scenario denies the currency of any metaphorical phrasings of self-perception. There can be no mind's eye, no internal insight or image of the Self. In the era of automated sight, human perception will compete with a computational construal of the environment. In this context the AT&T Long Lines Building should be appraised. Within its manifold cores, virtual worlds flash and perish at the speed of data transfer. 'The new monument,' Scott Bukatman comments: 'is no longer the substantial spatiality of the building, but the depthless surface of the screen'.[13] The screen as template of 'coded impulses' (Virilio) becomes the interface for virtual perception. Unpicturable, it is information on the move – the raw material of virtuality. Whether one conceives the notion of machine as assemblage of silicon and metal or fusion of neural-chemical processes and micro-robot, the theoretical implications necessarily remodel the means we have inherited to define what exactly is human about the human. One unifying factor shared among the painters considered in this essay is that they each reflect upon the altered territory of individuality conveyed through selected methods of mark-making. Each painter produces painting with the awareness that it will only be able to reveal and defend a subjectivity that transpires in reference to an alternative. The brushstroke, an apparent leitmotif of individuality, has in all cases been critically treated. With Dona the brush must shuttle between full-blown narrative regions and rudimentary linear diagrams; with Marcaccio exegesis of a magnified, corpulent stroke is a propositional process that can barely survive the ground on which it undulates. These examples of how painting can no longer adhere to prescribed methods, configure abstraction at a juncture of cognisant possibility – tempered by a criticality suspicious of delivering proclamations about an autonomy of subjectivity . . . for 'image feedback is no longer assured'.

Painting, the artists treated here intone, is profoundly concerned with the revelation of a contingency that will propel the immanent connections between intelligence and its Other.

The painted object is not preoccupied with a new relativism nor rhetoricism (the superficial strategies of Post-Modern pastiche and appropriation), but rather with the full realisation and re-evaluation of the terms of which the connections consist.

To situate this programme of diverse capacity, we regard the language of Artificial Intelligence to grasp how adeptly it has colonised the language of culture, biology, and philosophical humanism. Computer scientist Raymond Kurzweil limns the requisite complexity of what is entailed by 'Building a Brain' from a computational perspective. The concern here is with fabricating a cognisant entity that properly emulates the functionality of the human mind:

> Clearly, we need a capacity for hundreds of levels of parallel computations (with the parallelism of each stage potentially in the billions). The levels cannot be fully *self-organizing*, although the algorithms will in some cases allow for 'growing' new interneuronal connections. Each level will *embody* an algorithm, although the algorithms must permit *learning*. The algorithms are implemented in two ways: the transformations performed by the neurons themselves and the architecture of how the neurons are connected. The multiple layers of parallel neuronal analysis permit information to be encoded on *multiple levels of abstraction*. For example, in *vision*, images are first analyzed in terms of edges; edges form surfaces; surfaces form objects; objects form scenes. [emphasis added][14]

Highlighted parts of this description may obviously be likened to specific qualities of the human, roughly designating the realms of intelligence, innovation, and biological 'growth' (ie evolution). This model suggests how the human brain processes information at 'multiple levels of abstraction', situating that feature at the summa of neuronal performance. The belief underlying the project implies that the parallel-processing of mathematical algorithms may eventually come to replicate, if not surpass human abilities. Such an approach is known as strong AI or the computational approach to mind. It maintains unbridled confidence in selective paradigm processing where even the most complex or equivocal constructs can be tackled because they may be parsed, or mathematically written in terms of their 'formal representational structure'.[15]

John Searle, a cognitive scientist and philosopher who has consistently criticised strong AI strategies like the one above, notes that a digital machine, irrespective of its computational power, will be unable to exhibit traits such as 'intentionality' and 'consciousness', precisely because its operations can only be specified formally. A computer can only manipulate pre-ascribed abstract symbols that have no inherent value; the system constitutes a syntax but comprises no semantic – thus it can never know what it is doing.[16]

It is here that the philosophical debate within Artificial Intelligence blazes. The question 'can a machine think?' (that is, could a machine eventually think for itself and perform

FROM ABOVE: Helmut Dorner, Mas, 1994, 3 parts: lacquer and oil on plexiglass, 62 x 37 x 6cm, lacquer and oil on plexiglass, 45 x 34 x 9cm, lacquer on canvas and wood, 165 x 46 x 9 cm; Fabian Marcaccio, Paint Zone L.A. #2, 1995, collograph,oil on canvas, copper tubing and rope, 292 x 330 x 35.5cm

tasks such as interpreting an abstract painting), implicates a range of issues that even within the precincts of AI have yet to be addressed with a consistent terminology and methodology that would enable advocates and opponents to determine whether present-day computers exhibit characteristics such as 'introspection', 'mind', and 'self'. Ontological features are considered by critics of Artificial Intelligence (Searle and Hubert Dreyfus being the most prominent), to lie beyond the scope of simulation or replication at any level of digital computing.

From an objectivist, or strong AI vantage point, however, topics such as the Self obtain status as merely being one among the plethora of topics being accessed by machinic manipulation. Marvin Minsky, co-founder of the Media Laboratory at MIT and inveterate practitioner of the computational approach, conceives the notion of Self as specific to the system in which it operates. In his book *The Society of Mind*, that treats seemingly every conceivable aspect of the human as a discrete data-entry within a massively inter-linked system, Minsky configures the Self not as an abstract constant of the human identity. Rather, he discerns the Self within 'a vast constructed crust', acquiring resolution through its position within a given system. Here Self is associated with the example of painting:

> Why try to frame the value of a Self in a singularly frozen form? The art of a great painting is not in any one idea, nor in a multitude of separate tricks for placing all of those pigment spots, but in the great network of relationships among its parts. Similarly, the agents, raw, that make our minds are by themselves as valueless as aimless, scattered daubs of paint. What counts is what we make of them.[17]

This indeed seems a persuasive appraisal, even if it is reductionist, or single-minded in intent. The method of thinking is a portrait of rational, logical inference par excellence.

Why not pry apart the discernable components of each painting to attain a suitable 'network', parse discrete sets of attributes with which to constitute the painting? Certain painters here could be considered as emblematic – especially the work of Jonathan Lasker. His painting operates with codified separate parts, each strictly defined in terms of its boundaries, tactile constitution, and formal properties. Each part pronounces an independent, elemental character that cannot be confused with any other part. For example, a brushstroke would never be mistaken for a line; texture is always conceived as carefully apportioned quantity, occurring in designated forms and absent from the ground. This methodical mode of building a painting is supremely modular. Through the explication of his restricted means of formulating visual expression, Lasker mounts a critique of reductionism. Each of his works maintains the epiphany that the sum of the parts of any given painting can never (re)constitute the proper whole. The inter-relationships between the constituent elements multiply the possibilities with which lapidary connections can be made. The plan of Lasker's paintings is deliberately simplified so as to magnify this basic insight: the impossibility of designing a whole through assembly of its parts.

Helmut Dorner may similarly be regarded as escalating this approach to painting – the postulating of sequestered parts as configuring an extended whole. In *Mas* the work unfolds over three elements, each defined by distinctive material qualities. Where one panel is painted with lacquer on canvas, another uses oil paint and lacquer applied to plexiglass. The differences among these selected means scales internal and external properties of painting, retreating inwards to a system and extending out in reference to the wall and beyond. Spatially, variations of the panels' depth produce a curvature to perception, one which must overcome the intervals between the panels and estimate discrepancies between difference.

The parts are autonomously created and only brought indissolubly together after they have been painted. This strategy offers an example of a unity that begins and evolves along no preordained plane, but is rather an intuitive and integral configuration of a newly coalesced formation. The painting comes to demonstrate a kind of self-organising principle that openly ponders its own question of where it begins and where it may end. The rhythm to this opening is given by the cadence of the painting, a process of caesura that governs recognition.

This method foregrounds definitions of how perception and cognition diverge from each other; there is a distinct relationship although no explicit formula. These proximate polarities give rise to renewed levels of difference. The hovering quality of the paint applied only to the upper portion of the plexiglass panel causes perception to float, both into the surfaces themselves (probing notions of depth and opacity) and along the boundaries of the painting. Gradual attainment of the unity is experientially linked to a successive re-positioning of the viewing body. Conception, the painting suggests, differs fundamentally from its resultant apperception. Such a structured, yet non-systemic model is concerned with how the mind works, how it might come into contact with articulate configurations that appear to bear a casual (not causal) relationship with each other. The painting of tangible parts should not make closed what is not closed, or open what is not open.

Research in Artificial Intelligence can directly profit from the paradigmatic stance. The logical approach to modelling vision began with fixed, analogical thinking: 'computer scientists initially focused on vision in the belief that it would be easy to model: just start with the retinal image and recode it until you recover objects. That . . . turned out to be anything but easy'.[18] Such a task, of creating a machine with functional visual capacities commensurate to the human, can no longer viably adhere to a positivist, formalist agenda, even if this practice still comprises much contemporary research.[19] Recall the computational prescription for computer vision cited above: 'images are first analyzed in terms of edges; edges form surfaces; surfaces form objects; objects form scenes.' Here the underlying assumption is that visual cognition be-longs to the internal domain of the eye/brain/mind, and that the external environment is fixed.

Only very recently has this dogma been questioned within the AI community. Senior cognitive scientist Ulric Neisser has outlined the passage required, calling for a move away from identification and classification toward 'orientation', towards 'ecological perception'. The motivating component for Neisser's new approach is the human body, defined both in terms of its qualifiable processes and behavioral potential.

Despite ambitious projects and headstrong predictions of decades ago, computer systems today remain virtually blind when it comes to perceiving and interpreting the visible environment. Human seeing includes two distinct functions, each involving merged, distinct neural systems. *Orientation* enables us to see how the environment is configured and where we are spatially located in it. *Recognition* concerns how we manage to correlate objects or symbols with internal representations and thus identify what we see. Mastering these functions has proven a major obstacle to computers. Although systems have success in processing artificial phenomena (magnetic letters, bar codes, printed text, etc), they remain blind to the world and therefore void of orientation.

Neisser, following the perceptual psychologist JJ Gibson, argues against the representationist model of perception. What we see is not the signal in the optic nerve but the real environmental situation, and how we understand the visual world is directly governed by the scale and abilities of our bodies. The environment has a structure independent of our needs. We do not see our environment by processing information from which it can be inferred (represented), but by picking up objectively existing information that uniquely specifies the visible world for our active bodies.[20] Calling this process 'direct perception', it may be thought of as an ecological model of perception. 'The understanding of vision,' Neisser adduces, 'requires a description of the world at the level of visible things'.[21] As a model, it demands the necessity that vision, if it is to contain meaning, must involve a 'co-perception of environment and self'.[22]

The twinning of these core components returns us to the fundamental disparity between the machine and the human. With the prescription of environment and self, the task of Artificial Intelligence designs itself again as desirous of building artificial perception upon the example of human perceptual processes. Even with of the ecological infusion of 'direct perception' proposed by Neisser, the project is fundamentally coded, and thus reducible in essence to the aims of simulation – to reliance upon the human as model to be replicated. Yet it has been precisely through the artificial opening up of the body by telematic manipulation, that its relative scale to the world has passed away from our capacities of visualisation.

This narrative of dysfunctional union is played out in the work of Lydia Dona, where urban ecology is thrust into scalar affiliation with the human body. In her *Occupants Within The*

Gaze On The Nerves Of Urban Tissues (see page 86) the interface between visual and architectural enterprises acquires antagonistic furore.[23] The painting is segmented or traversed by sequences of parallel lines which map the surface into sections, the enunciated gridding of metropolitan space. Or, these girding lines refer to architectural *blue*prints, proffering information about zoning, urban planning, or the structural composition of buildings. Into this linear, overlaid grid, a conical pyramid sweeps downwards, tracing a visual arc that illuminates the ground of the painting in an eerie yellow wash. Like a search beam this wan light traces the scope of the gaze. That there may be 'Occupants' within this evacuated space appears contradictory, until the shape is seen to extend (behind the cornea?) along to the upper right corner of the painting. In this upward, reflected zone of the conical visual pyramid, a panoply of machinic diagramming occurs. It is these linear, instructional, motor components that become the 'Occupants'. They power the vision of shape to see literally through the environment of the painting; through its blue ground, beneath the linear gridding of urban space. If sight becomes the void into which the gaze travels, then this vision is dependant upon machinery residing above the gaze – working to fabricate sight.

Around the periphery of the projected gaze, the painting conducts its neuronal, cellular activity – the production of 'Urban Tissues'. Multichromed chemical fluids meander through boundary lines, clouding the sectioned space of the painting and combining with high-keyed pointillist drippings of enamel paint. Patchy regions of a darker, brush-laid blue appear beside the conical gaze, and a magenta assembly of cells proliferate along the bottom of the painting, below the gaze. These manifestations stimulate the 'Nerves Of Urban Tissues' combining to agitate production of vision's space. The synthesis of neural networks with architecture – meshing the corporeal with machinic assemblies – gives rise to a model of painting (and self) that slips into the territory of visionary science.

When Donna Haraway, a historian of science and biology, defines 'mind as the strategy of genes'[24], she places the human organism into a mechanistic frame of evolutionary progress radically open for alteration. In her genetics of behaviour, whereby the 'natural economy [proceeds] according to capitalist relations,' intervention becomes the figure for increased efficiency and quality: 'there is no logical, much less moral, barrier to a full engineering approach to outmoded systems'.[25] The 'system' may be the human organism (with its limited faculties such as vision), but when placed in the frame of sociobiology, a larger scope is mandated. The gene becomes merely a machinic quantum shared by classes of manufactured organisms (systems). Alerting us to the reality that when one speaks of 'gene' or 'computer', organic associations have passed into the realms of engineering, statistical control and the communications sciences along Haraway's line, the fabrication of the life-sciences moves towards augmentation. There are no

longer any singularities, no individuums – there is merely the prototype that will inaugurate a new manufacturing line.

If painting is to stand in resistance to this ineluctible plan, it must do so less by assertion of its craft, than by throwing up a theoretical model recalcitrant to co-optation. *Paint Zone L.A. #2* by Fabian Marcaccio produces such a model, presenting a 'prototype' impossible to replicate. The genetics of his proposition are given by the display of extreme magnification. The code of painting is broken into its 'least elements' (Haraway), in this case: pigment, weave, ground, stroke, splash. Here, however, there is no texture, only the intangible figment of its semblance – a diversionary tactic. The actual surface of the canvas is serenely smooth, with all of the shadows and haptic features of the weave being colour fluctuations rather than sequences of any overlaid stroke. The entire image – which traces the birth of a painting from tumescent ground, to finely woven ground, to fabric assembling into form, brushstroke, splash, seepage – is seamlessly printed or screened onto the canvas. If the brush has been applied at all, then its furtive manoeuvres have mingled imperceptibly into the paint itself, absorbed into the diverse patterning. In this planar, illusory environment the only real shadows (differentiation of trace and form) are those thrown beyond the canvas itself.

Over a copper-pipe scaffolding, which is a support as much as space modulating device, the canvas has been stretched. Its actual distance from the wall, measured by the numerous extensions of rope, is given by the copper piping – a bizarre metallic substructure. If the surface and image of the painting narrates a micro-biology wherein the promotion of mutation is paramount, beneath and beyond the surface, the metabolism of the object rephrases this mandate. Painting-as-object risks becoming a banner strapped to a wall, rigged under high tension and prepared to defend itself as suggested by its metallic armature (note how the silver paint deflects light).

Marcaccio's *Paint Zone L.A. #2* – classified by place and number – escalates the notion of hybridisation. Perceptually the painting evades the methodology of vision. The scale and span of the work explodes any relation to Self defined through the corporeality of human sight – commuting from echelons of intense magnification to full-blown urban situations. By introducing a metropoliptic metaphor into the work's programme, Marcaccio sprawls the image through diverse connotational territory. In terms of the city, the painting proposes an alternative method of habitation or spatial occupation. It refuses to conventionally hang on the wall, but may rather be likened to an entity squatting within the gallery space. Its protuberant surface hovers in front of the wall, presses into our space and in so doing refuses to be absorbed and neutralised. It would seem to number among those 'Others' who comprise the disenfranchised segments of the urban population outside the corporate-based economy. If one were to use the grid as signifier of the global metropolitan economy, as Saskia Sassen has[26], then Marcaccio's painting would clearly fall outside this sign. *Paint Zone L.A. #2* conceives the metropolis as void of the grid, replete with a bulging intensity that is a de-structuring, lesioning portrayal of self-doubt. The rupture delivered by painting questions all of its emblematic methods, such fundaments as brush use and canvas support. Acute subjectivity becomes the consequence of this urban/paint zone – an experience provoked by the city yet unmappable by any of its institutional structures. It is in this manner that another narrative tier is added to the discourse on vision – where seeing must carry with it the responsibilities of human consciousness.

In writing about abstraction and its intercourse with present technologies of the information age, John Rajchman situates painting as being able to discern '"abstract" virtualities of other things.' Following from Deleuze, painting, like cinema, would press towards messages unfolding beyond the inherent constraints of its medium, ever connecting to an Outside. 'For this *world* is what abstraction is all about,' Rajchman concludes: 'abstraction as the attempt to show – in thought as in art, in sensation as in concept – the odd multiple unpredictable potential in the midst of things, of other new things, other new mixtures'.[27] Yet, as our place in this world is redefined, connections acquire an interactivity at levels that never before existed. Consider the example of nano-machines, soon to be introduced into the body, into its bloodstream to enhance or redesign our natural abilities to fight off infection. 'Here are the final prostheses, the new automatons,' Virilio dubs the micro-robot: 'ANIMATORS that will populate our organism, just as we ourselves have populated and arranged the entire body of the earth.'[28] Implemented perhaps, in the form of a capsule to be swallowed, the abstraction involved becomes one difficult to picture: '*intelligent pills* capable of transmitting at a distance information about the nervous system and blood flow . . .'[29] Here we find the revolutionary science of the information age, machines fusing seamlessly with cellular biology, united in a mutual effort of information exchange. The *abstract* reworking demanded by this model – communicated by the painting of Dona and Marcaccio – reconfigures not merely how, but more precisely where, we might locate the understanding of intelligence. Such an 'intelligent pill' (containing micro-machines) does not enhance intelligence as we currently know it (the consciousness of brain processes), but would in fact constitute a form of intelligence. Fittingly, this would surely give rise to 'other new things, other new mixtures' – the project of abstraction.

In the painting of Chuck Close abstraction receives tangible articulation through the presence of representation. The contingency of these categories, their mutually-bound proximity, is determined through the degree of information accorded units within the painting. The scalar shift required for articulation between these terms spans Virilio's frame of the corporeal – from animator to organism. Close's image evades the scale of our bodies appearing at once over-large and minute. This bi-

valent schema of presentation, that recedes infinitely within itself narrates the form that information occupies. As data and flow, paint here becomes the analogue for digital technology.

When Norbert Wiener, the founder of cybernetics, mused that 'the distinction between material transportation and message transportation is not in any theoretical sense permanent or unbridgeable'[30], he speculated on a moment of transcendental communication that not only dispenses with the conventional logic of space but with corporeal coordinates of location (Gottmann's inevitable fungible space). For Wiener, writing in 1951, the human organism was conceivable as a sequence of patterns, similar to the way genetics parses any organism. If a pattern is discernable, then it may be coded as a message – information tractable for transmission:

> We are not stuff that abides, but patterns that perpetuate themselves . . . consider what would happen if we were to transmit the whole pattern of the human body, of the human brain with its memories and cross-connections, so that a hypothetical receiving instrument could re-embody these messages in appropriate matter, capable of continuing the processes already in the body and the mind, and of maintaining the integrity needed for this continuation by processes of homeostasis.[31]

Painting may be considered such a 'hypothetical receiving instrument,' suitable for reconfiguring a transmitted human body and mind. If Wiener envisioned devices akin to computers, scanners, and video-linked televisions then, simply the means of his insight differ from those of painting. Painting is communication; it represents an advanced state of human expression as transmission, for in it the identity of subjectivity is both specified and perpetuated.

Identity may be read as central to Close's painting. In his fingerprint works, from the 1970s and 1980s, the paint was applied through the touch of his finger to canvas – each 'stroke' an impression of the artist's unique hand. Such incessant individuation, carried with the brush through more recent works such as *Paul*, describes the complexity required of Wiener's 'continuing the processes already in the body and the mind.' Close's painting projects our sight across expanses of gallery and museum spaces. If at close range the image breaks apart into a near-anarchic 'Paint-Zone', with distance, the information reformats itself into the articulate picture of a face. The painting allows us to see information clearly, to behold 'homeostatic' data at various distances. Close's image is both fixed yet still seeming to undergo processes of information transmission/ reception. The allegory of Polke's *The Computer Moves In* is experienced as actually transpiring in the Close painting, where intercourse with virtuality is a consequence of *our* viewing, rather than that of a depicted figure's.

Such a consciousness decodes the surfeit of invisible information flowing through our constructed environment and selves. It interposes sequences of subjective attainment, as

FROM ABOVE: Chuck Close, Paul, 1994, oil on canvas, 259 x 213cm; work in progress; detail (photos, Ellen Page Wilson)

interpretation, within the labile, constantly shifting spatiality of the city. In speaking about the polyphony that experience of the contemporary metropolis has become, Félix Guattari discerns an interminable 'partial subjectivity: the city, the street, the building, the door, the hall – each itself and in composition a centre of subjectivation.'[32] Close's painting endeavours to deliver mobile parameters which enable the whole to maintain value within discrete units of subjectivation. Each quadrant within the painting's diagonal grid constitutes an identic image.

In Close's environment the grid is rotated, detached from any perspectival association and given independent structural iteration, creating an infinite dimensionality to flatness. There is an intrinsic, morphological tie between human identity and inhabited space. A distant unit of ground, when compared to a facial feature, is invested with the same paint-information and yields the same attentive span of the brush, thus collapsing any figure/ground division. Space is charged with meaning, activated into the de-neutralised territory of information and given machinic placement within painting's structure, to use Guattari's phrasing:

> The span of developed/constructed space extends quite beyond their visible and functional structures. They are essentially machines, machines of meaning, of sensation, abstract machines . . . that carry incorporeal universes that are not universals but that can standardize individual and collective subjectivity.[33]

This model concerning a 'subjectivation of space' services the urban environment and that of painting. Within these realms, carrying 'incorporeal universes', information transfer mediates to construct a 'collective subjectivity'. Intelligibility, or integrity (Wiener's term), becomes the ledger of information's transmission, enabling placement within the structures we have built.

All discourses in AI converge here, along the episteme of the human; the human as inclusive definition, from self to cell, cultured creature to constructed machine. Beyond any visible, functional delineation, the space of painting machinically fabricates meaning. Whether comprised of Zones or Urban Tissues, pixelated quadrants or windows into which we look, the scalar shifts not only become the site of intelligence's purview but chase opticality through all levels of subjectivation.

Any mind, so long as it inhabits the body will perpetuate a formally conscious continuity to subjectivity, for that is the reference to which it relates. The spectrum of artists presented here details this arc – the body at the limits of its prospects, where from such limits a propositional intelligence might begin to take up the responsibility of Being beyond the corporeal. Only once we move beside an anthropomorphic model for creation will Other implications for intelligence (artificial or not) be attained.

If the prevalent assumption today is that 'the driving force in the growth of machine intelligence will continue to be human intelligence, at least for the next 50 years'[31], then, it should be beyond this time-frame, beyond progress to interface and integration that we should look for a real non-human intelligence. The ultimate thinking machine would evolve an independence where it can fully dismantle its connections to anthropomorphic intelligence and exist free of corporeal constraints, a thought we are perhaps slow in realising. In the shadow of the AT&T Long Lines Building, however, the scope of this project is tangibly articulated.

If, as eminent science fiction writer Arthur C Clarke says, 'real intelligence won't be living', perhaps it is away from the phenomenal definition of Self and rather to an Other that we should move. Every description of painting aims to bring it towards life, into our world – to make it speak so as to allow us to see into its core, an essence. Perhaps that is not at all what the paintings record. For later on, much later, none of these objects as images will be known as painting. Merely, they will seem to intelligence to be previous models of mind – the enshrined architecture into which Being once walked.

Notes

A version of this essay originally appeared in the catalogue accompanying the exhibition *Architecture of the Mind*, curated by myself at Galerie Barbara Farber, Amsterdam, 22 April – 24 May, 1995. I am grateful to Barbara Farber for the opportunity provided by that exhibition to develp my thoughts on the relationship between abstract painting and artificial intelligence.

1 Interview with Arthur C Clarke by Gene Youngblood and Ted Zatlyn in Gene Youngblood, *Expanded Cinema*, Dutton, New York, 1970, p149. Clarke, with Stanley Kubrick, co-authored the script for *2001: A Space Odyssey* in which the autonomous computer HAL 9000 made its debut.

2 See Paul Goldberger, *The City Observed: New York, A Guide to the Architecture of Manhattan*, Vintage, New York, 1979, p39. Caption information is derived from *Architectural Record*, July 1969, pp123-30.

3 Jean Gottmann, 'Urban Settlements and Telecommunications', in *Since Megalopolis: the Urban Writings of Jean Gottman*, The John Hopkins University Press, Baltimore, 1990, pp39-40.

4 Charles Jencks, *The Language of Post-Modern Architecture*, Academy Editions, London, 1991, p194.

5 Gottmann, 'Urban Settlements . . .', p199.

6 Gary Chapman, 'Taming the Computer', in *Flame Wars: The Discourse of Cyberculture*, Mark Dery (ed), *South Atlantic Quarterly*, Vol 92, No 4, (Fall 1993), p831, p834.

7 Marvin Minsky, 'Thoughts about Artificial Intelligence', in *The Age of Intelligent Machines*, Raymond Kurzweil (ed), MIT Press, Cambridge, MA, 1990, p214.

8 Some of the specialised research fields of this discipline are: pattern recognition, expert systems, automatic theorem proving, cognitive psychology, word processing, machine vision, knowledge engineering, symbolic applied mathematics, and computational linguistics.

9 Bernard Tschumi, *Architecture and Disjunction*, MIT Press, Cambridge, MA, 1994, p21.

10 See for example, *Cyberspace: First Steps*, Michael Benedikt, ed, MIT Press, Cambridge, MA, 1991 and *Culture, Technology and Creativity in the Late Twentieth Century*, Philip Hayward (ed), John Libbey & Co, London, 1990.

11 Margaret A Boden, *Artificial Intelligence in Psychology: Interdisciplinary Essays*, MIT Press, Cambridge, MA, 1989, p48.

12 Paul Virilio, *The Vision Machine*, Indiana University Press, Bloomington, 1994, p73.

13 Scott Bukatman, *Terminal Identity: The Virtual Subject in Postmodern Science Fiction*, Duke University Press, Durham, 1993, p132.

14 Raymond Kurzweil, *The Age of Intelligent Machines*, MIT Press, Cambridge, MA, 1990, p233.

15 See Roy Eagleson, 'Computations Over Abstract Categories of Representation', in *Behavioral and Brain Sciences*, Vol 13, no 4, (1990), p662. For an appraisal of Strong AI programs such as the OSCAR system of automated reasoning, see John L Pollock, 'OSCAR: A General Theory of Rationality', in *Philosophy and AI: Essays at the Interface*, Robert Cummins and John Pollock (eds), MIT Press, Cambridge, MA, 1991, pp189-213.

16 See John Searle, *Minds, Brains and Science*, Harvard University Press, Cambridge, MA, 1984, pp30-31ff. More recently Searle has reiterated this point: notions such as computation, algorithm, and program do not name intrinsic physical features of systems. Computational states are not discovered . . . they are assigned.' See Searle, *The Rediscovery of the Mind*, MIT Press, Cambridge, MA, 1992, p210.

17 Marvin Minsky, *The Society of Mind*, Simon & Schuster, New York, 1985, p41.

18 Ulric Neisser, 'Without Perception, There Is No Knowledge: Implications for Artificial Intelligence', in *Natural and Artificial Minds*, Robert G Burton, ed, State University of New York Press, Albany, 1993, p154.

19 The Project List from MIT's Media Laboratory reveals the extent of research dedicated to perceptual computing. Fully one-third of the roughly 100 research projects are perceptual in orientation. See *Project List*, Media Laboratory, Massachusetts Institute of Technology, September 8, 1993.

20 'Human perceptual orientation . . . depends chiefly on the pickup of the deeply interlocked information structures made available by movement, structures that unequivocally specify both the layout of the environment and the perceiver's own position'. Neisser, 'Without Perception . . . ,' p163. The complexities of 'self-world interactions involving perceptual experience' have recently been investigated by Shigeko Takahashi, 'Aesthetic Properties of Pictorial Perception', *Psychological Review*, Vol 102, No 4 (1995), pp671-83.

21 Neisser, *ibid*, p154.

22 *ibid*, p156.

23 I have developed this theme in greater detail in 'Lydia Dona: Architecture of Anxiety', in *Journal of Philosophy and The Visual Arts: Abstraction*, Andrew Benjamin (ed), (No 5), Academy Editions, 1995, pp43-51.

24 Donna J Haraway, 'The Biological Enterprise: Sex, Mind, and Profit from Human Engineering to Sociobiology', in *Simians, Cyborgs, and Women: The Reinvention of Nature*, Routledge, London, 1991, p63.

25 *ibid*, p 66; preceding quote p68.

26 See Saskia Sassen, 'Analytic Borderlands: Economy and Culture in the Global City', in *Columbia Documents of Architecture and Theory*, Vol 3, 1993, pp5-22.

27 John Rajchman, 'Another View of Abstraction', in *Journal of Philosophy and the Visual Arts*, op cit, p22.

28 Paul Virilio, 'The Law of Proximity', in *D: Columbia Documents of Architecture and Theory*, Vol 2, 1993, pp123-24.

29 *ibid*, p124.

30 Norbert Wiener, *The Human Use of Human Beings: Cybernetics and Society*, Da Capo Press, New York, 1950, p98.

31 *ibid*, p96.

32 Félix Guattari, 'Space and Corporeity', in *D: Columbia Documents of Architecture and Theory*, Vol 2, 1993, pp143-44.

33 *ibid*, p145.

34 Kurzweil, *The Age of Intelligent Machines*, p463.

Crisis in Western Representation, *1992, acrylic on canvas, 114.3 x 88.9cm*

SUSPENSION OF DISBELIEF
THE BODY OF THE PAINTER IN THE FACE OF THE VIRTUAL
Robert Yarber

What is certain is that believing is no longer believing in another world, or in a transformed world. It is only, it is simply, believing in the body.[1]

Suspension of Disbelief . . . we are out there, hanging, suspended, lost in space. The partitions are falling between the real and the illusory at rapidly accelerating rates. I'm signalling you. You're signalling me. We wave at each other across the solipsistic chasm, as horizon lines tilt towards a primal 'hermetic core'. If language 'speaks' us, then pictures 'pose' us. We are props in a grand *mise en scène*. The vaulting sky enshrouds our hurtling bodies.

The painter believes in the body. 'The painter takes his body with him,' says Valéry. But this knocked around, over-exposed, generic body seeks respite, and whispers 'Don't paint me, let me disappear'. 'Where?' you ask, 'Where aren't there bodies?'. The virtual real estate gets used up as terrestrial fantasies become finite, confining. The Lascaux bison must have inevitably become a bore. What to draw now? Outside the cave arches the infinite firmament, but how to draw it?

Humanity has always struggled with its desire to escape from the body.

The history of art is the history of the body. Our embodiment within the virtual space of the imaginary is made manifest in traditional modes of creative expression. With painting playing a principal role, the imaginary becomes concretised within the image. Lived body becomes effigy. For the ancients, these effigies were still sentient. For us they have become symbolic. The nostalgia for the speaking statues and weeping paintings lingers however, and a return to idols is under way via cyberspace. As the body gets sucked into the virtual, our belief in its reality becomes more fragile. The derealisation of the body will effect broad realignments in the social and cultural spheres, redefining the concepts of work and leisure, and no doubt, penury. In this process will the history of art get morphed off the map?

The urge to revirtualise the imaginary within phantasmic worlds is ever renewed as the vivacity of the reality effect projected through the lens of the virtual grows dim. Living virtuality becomes dead virtuality, as the 'real' vampirises itself through ever more elaborate transfusions of technical innovation. Spectatorship is taking us somewhere . . . it might not be good for us, but it feels great. As virtual space goes dead – gets used up – more of the body, and more of the soul, must stand in reserve to await deployment. If the painter takes his body with him as Valéry suggests, it is over scarred ground, littered with other painters' bodies. The battle for the reality effect is waged on many fronts, painting being but one skirmish along a long line of conflict. Yet it is a fundamental site in the overall theatre of virtualisation. The act of painting, very recently having been relegated to the trashbin of history, is attracting scavengers.

The painter's body is an obscene engine of virtuality, as the history of art attests. The projection of the reality effect – a manifestation of the imaginary perceived through the veils of the symbolic – demands the sacrifice of the body, the real, for its double. The melding of the painting and the body of the painter is a dry run for artists readying themselves for the body-gloves of virtual reality.

The Corporeal Theatre

The presentation of the painter's body before the canvas is an act of display, an act of mirroring. The body becomes face[2], it is frontalised, ocularised, before the nascent scene. Whether the painting is flat or on an easel, does not matter. As the blind are said to experience a kind of 'facial sight', so the painter experiences a kind of body sight, like radar. His body is open for the painting, naked and transparent. This opening is a conjunction of sorts; the painter has sent out virtual nerves to the canvas, the body and painting comprising a kind of monadic entelechy; an environmental, space. The introduction of a tool, any tool (brush, spray, camera, torch, etc) into this morphogenetic space creates a lesion which must heal, so that the nerve-rays of the body-painting can reconnect. Much has been said about paint as flesh (as in the work of Bacon for example), but this phrase has been understood too metaphorically. The danger of painting, to the jeopardy and pleasure of the painter, is that this enfibrillation of painterly and bodily flesh is literally real, on the level of the virtual. An evisceration of the body proper (the biological organism) must take place to empower the virtualisation that will empower this transubstantiation. The production of this expenditure is key in our understanding of the desire for virtuality.

This environment – shared by the painter's body and its object of desire, the painting – comprises a kind of Nature, or more rightly a nature reserve, for there are other natures and other love objects encompassing other terrain, and other denizens of the virtual (the aural, olfactory, etc). However, the regional ontology of the painting can be understood as seamless within itself, unbifurcated or riven by symbol or sign. One can live and breathe deeply in the realm of the virtual. Usually for about a nanosecond. The presentness of presence is fleeting.

The dematerialisation of the body in the Act of painting is attained through the body's occupation of a vitalised, virtual space, a virtual hole in the real. The threshold of recognition through which the body casts its ray enframes the body. The window effect depends on the passing through. The eye must cast the body forth, suspending and projecting the virtual body along its ocular ray. The aperture, or threshold into the virtual, must be passed. It must be understood that the window is in the body, somehow eviscerating it, (as with the Schreberian body[3]). The body – thus passing through itself – must be enframed, first by the threshold, then its beyond. The body must hang suspended in the beyond.

Body Degree Zero

Just as noetically a *ray of love* proceeding from the Ego *splits up into a bundle of rays*, each of which is directed towards a single object, so too there are distributed over the collective object of affection as such as many noemetic characters of love as there are objects collected at that time.[4]

The facialised, ocularised, body of the painter confronts its mirror-image in the scene of the painting. Two poles of attraction are established in a 'seance' during which the body of the painter hangs suspended within the world of the scene, in a stilled moment within which the body is levitated, weightless and floating, within the diaphanous substance pervading the osmotic field of regard. Settled within its projection, the body is the '*nullpunkt*' or zero-point of origin that is nonetheless compelled to send itself out within the sphere of its own self-reflection. This projection founds the habitat of a provisional, virtualised world, a recursive feed-back scenography in which the pulse of protention and retention support a fragile 'now'. The superflux of the sensate is stalled down within a congealed, Medusean prolapsus of the stare. A still world.

This analogue world becomes, fleetingly, a mirage of the 'ground of grounds' in the Husserlian sense of being the primordial resting place of the here. So, this counterfeit here of virtual space is the prolapse of some real here only dimly perceived but actively desired. This desired world would not move but in fact know:

the rest of an absolute here, a rest which is not the rest of the object (rest as a 'mode of motion'), but Rest starting from which motion and rest can appear and be thought of as such, the Rest of a ground and a horizon in their common origin and end.[5]

This dual pseudo-primordiality of virtualised body and world cohabit a molecular precinct of apperception within which the reality effect is burlesqued and savoured. The mirrorisation of the painter's body within the landscape of the scene is not in fact visual, but purely visceral. This is the blind spot of the gaze, the pass through which the root of the gaze drives itself. It is sensible to think of the gaze as hermaphroditic in this respect; as it couples with itself in the interior and anterior convolutions of its self-consumption.

Two mirrors face each other. Facing mirrors send simulacral segmentations of themselves one into the heart of the other, each searching for an infinitely recessive point of return. This cascading ray of enframents would carry a hypothetical observer on a boundless journey. Likewise, the body of the painter sends forth templates into the mirror world, its visceral inner frames forming exoskeletons; each a mirror, each a still point along a prehensile train traversing a medium reverberating with the charge of somatic recognition. Where in Kappers' Law nervous structures defined as associated in action become associated in position, in the virtualised body, sensations of the proprioceptive organs are channelled into penumbras of imaginary or would-be action. Through the false cues presented for motor-sensory response in the somatic recognition of the perpetually de- and re-virtualising body of the painter, it is posed, indeed played or pantomimed, before the scene. The scene of the painting becomes a homing-device or releasing-mechanism before which the body of the painter is hopelessly labile. At this point the disposition of the painter's body before the painting is distinctly involuntary. Here lies the scandal and danger, as well as the comedy of painting.

The act of painting is founded in the recursivity of this passive modulation in which feeling feels itself. The means to express the workings of this mechanics of the felt gaze were groped for in the metaphysics of ancient optics. Ancient optics provided numerous descriptions of the nature of visuality that are not merely of historical interest but serve as viable tools for identifying the disposition of the painter's body in the face of the painting. Psycho-podia, or limbs of the soul (Hipparchus), virtually reached out to retrieve the skin-like simulacra of the object of observation (Democritus and Epicurus). For the Platonists, the gaze opened up a line of transmission between the observer and the observed in which each sent forth attributes of light that intermixed along a diaphanous ray (Aristotle).[6]

I would like to suggest a model of vision combining the themes of extromission and intromission with regard to the engulfment of the painter's body within the scene of the painting in which the ocular body is projected forward towards its object as a generation of exploded homunculi, to retrieve the atom, simulacra, or skin of the scene. The poles are reversed as the effluence of homunculi is drawn off the body towards the scenic, the arc of homunculi streaming forth within the voluptuous suction. The space between the painter's body and its object is akin to the ancient substance, the translating media 'of air, water, or crystal'; the diaphanon. The shedding of the homunculi by the painter's ocularised body anticipates the synaesthetic modes of comportment that will be experienced within digitised virtual reality environments. The body glove will occupy a digitised, 'full', diaphanous dimension, any point of which can be concretised at will. Virtual reality is the setting of the beyond. This transactional space is vivified, or given life, through the expenditure of the shed skins or mirror-bodies of the painter.

The streaming forth of the homunculi, or skins of the body, constitutes the flesh of the visible. The space is open, viable. The threshold of recognition mirrors itself, a 'recollection of the present in the present'.[7] The picture plane is a 'slice of time'. The window effect or threshold of recognition emanating from the picture plane involves the painter in the spatialisation of time. The depicted scene is the still, the freeze frame, the unmoving, frozen world of the ancient Eleatic philosophy. The enframing of the picture moves forward towards the painter, it is projective, while at the same time it also remains, and likewise returns in a circular movement or circuit in a manner similar to that of spiritual motion as described by Neo-Platonist philosophers such as Proclus.[8] The more commonplace perusal of the scene takes place before and after this moment. This is the eye-lock of 'darkness visible'.[9]

The digitised environments of computer imaging programs such as 'Photoshop' provide interesting examples of the spatialisation of the temporal. The 'shot' or visible slice of time that comes up in the computer display of a photographic scene is transversable in a way that technically mimics the perusal mechanisms of vision, and quite similarly to that described by the ancient idea of psycho-podia. In fact, 'moving-tools' in the form of small, prehensile hand icons specifically recall the limbs of the soul that would go out to retrieve the simulacral objects of the seen world. These hand icons, such as the smearing thumb of the 'smudge tool', undermine and at the same time inculcate the reality effect within the scenic in a new, and quite subversive manner. In this program the 'painter' moves, brings forward or pushes back the 'shot' – or slice of time – of a stalled-down present that is transversable and deletable in strikingly new ways. A fine example of how the morbidity of the virtual can be revivified in eerie and somewhat macabre ways can be seen in the smearing of a simple verisimilitude such as a depicted tree with the 'smudge tool', which can be utterly obscured to the point of unrecognisability, and then revived, resurrected as it were, with a hit of the 'undo smudge' command.

The hits, clicks and commands of this new body of the painter certainly cast it forward into an ever more rarefied modality. The flesh of the visible becomes increasingly malleable and ever more 'realistic', at the same time as it is wrested from the need for any specific support structures such as canvas or photographic paper. The support can and will be anything, and ultimately may be found in the artificially enhanced functions of localised cortical regions, where the virtual can be most directly manipulated. How this new cortical region as canvas is augmented, by what weave and filigree of wave and ray, will

very soon become more clear. Whether the commercialised 'will-to-power' of technological revivifications of the real leads to the drunken orgy of visual mayhem so feared by critics, or to the birth of a new ocular body, bold in its grasp of the possibilities of expression, remains uncertain. And what other 'bodies', of which we are only the distant progenitors, will we meet 'in the flesh' as it were, at some future site of engagement?

The Mirror-World

'The "axis" of vision is, I suggest the line of greatest desire: a line imposed by the will to power.'[10]

The ocularisation of the body is symmetrically opposed to the disincarnation of the eye. The ocularisation of the body might be confused with the infamous and vilified disincarnated, monocular eye commonly mentioned in respect to the syndrome of the ocularcentrism in Western visuality.[11] This image, taken from Descartes' (and Kepler's) experiment with a sliced open cow's eye, has been described as a 'presenting' symptom of Western pathology. Identified with the Spectacle (Debord), the Show (Illich), the World-Picture (Heidegger), the visuality of the West is associated with the 'rebirth' of perspectival space as it was practiced in Renaissance painting. The privatising, rationalising, idealising function of theoretically rigorous perpectivalism represents the scopic regime of the West at its purest, and is said to have given rise in part to the isolated, disembodied subject as typified by the Cartesian ego. Here, the body is eviscerated by technique, by the instrumentalisation of mathematical space. The Cartesian subject looks out upon its body as an alien extension of the general field of available tools. The body and soul are irrevocably split, the body becomes machine; the soul, subject. This invention of Western space, of *res extensa*, is observed by the disembodied eye from afar. Space under the disembodied view is left uninhabitable. The idealised spatial grid superimposed over matter is approachable only by an immaterial ego. Therefore, space – in its scientific and metaphysical dimension – is evacuated by the soul, becoming a stage left empty for phantoms; a *vitrine* to be studied through glass.

'Technology, whose essence is Being itself, will never allow itself to be overcome by men'.[12]

The technologisation of the virtual seeks the overthrow of the real in its status as evacuated space. Modernity is born in the split between *res cognitans* and *res extensa*. Virtual space explodes as real space collapses into the quantum smear. Today, the utopian desire to reoccupy the real drives the virtual to Frankensteinian lengths. With a dream of retrieving, and reanimating the real, we plot to entomb the 'brain' of the reality effect (the subject), within the cadaver of the real. The radical contingency of the real (its death) will thus be overcome. The optical glove, the optical suit, are devices, prosthetics, apparati; as they are roots and tendrils of the real seeking to climb the ray of the virtual. Plotinus described this cleaving to of matter

FROM ABOVE: Sins of the Scopophilliacs, *1991, acrylic on canvas, 90.2 x 113.7cm;* The Imposters, *1989, oil on canvas, 182.9 x 335.3cm*

to soul, and of the soul's yearning for matter.[13] Does the real seek penetration into the virtual or visa versa?

The Baroque could be seen as a transhistorical response to notions of space that serve to evacuate it and deplete its habitability in the sense of its being the abode of souls. It was a reaction to this crisis in western spatiality. In its hysterical contortions of pictorial space, the Baroque requisitioned the sky for bodies. Space becomes infinitely inhabitable in the Roman Baroque ceiling just as 17th-century science was purging the body of its cosmological imprimatur. The Baroque presents the very model of a 'full', transactional virtual space that anticipates the explosion of the virtual later found in cinema, and more recently cyberspace. The Negative Baroque, to use the late Edward Fry's phrase, likewise would act as a reactive ideology forcing the reanimation of dying virtualities in the course of their social and historical failure. In truth the virtual is neither living nor dead. It is the undead. Alberti had seen perspectival space as being co-terminal with the space of *istoria*. As painters gradually lost faith in these stories, they sought to revive the pictorial through the libidinalisation of pictorial space itself. For Baroque, and especially Rococo painters such as Boucher and Fragonard, the story often becomes secondary to the depiction of a fulsome and supple, yet airy, almost pneumatic materiality in which the atmosphere itself is palpable. A revivification of the virtual is attempted in its own expenditure through the 'fetishization of space itself'.[14]

Themes of the resurrection of the real within the virtual can be found throughout Western tradition. In the medieval period the identification of the relic of the saint's body with both the body proper and the virtual body of its miraculous and Resurrected state, posed a dilemma for the theoretical concerns of the Church Fathers.[15] In the final hour of Resurrection, as conceived by some theories, the dispersed members of the saintly body, the finger joints, jaw bone, and dried blood, would fly up out of far flung reliquaries, and hurtle at God-speed across continents, to be recombined at last whole and restored. The importance placed on the idea of the intact body, and of the recombinant nature of its Resurrected state in medieval theology, provides curious analogies to the problems that will face cyborg morality as the penetration of the virtual within the real confuses ever further the parameters and very definition of 'life'.

The body of the Renaissance Magus was a fleshy talisman, a lure for superterrestrial correspondence. It was open lodging for passing daemonic influences, a microcosmic mirror held up to the stars. It was undermined, however, by Neo-platonic prejudice, which understood physical, worldly acts to be soul-besmirching errors. The Renaissance art theorist Lomazzo regarded the painter Raphael to be a demi-god. Regrettably, however, the artist had engaged in the physical act of painting, and in Lomazzo's opinion, the truly divine aspect of Raphael's vision was tarnished in its translation into material form. The persistence of Platonic and Neo-Platonic influences linger in our culture and in fact have become increasingly pronounced in literature regarding cyberspace, virtual reality, and the technologisation of the virtual. The effectiveness of a New Body brought forth in the futuristic scenarios common to virtual reality literature challenges the dreams of Paracelsus and Faust. But branching off the same root are the statements of various AI (artificial intelligence) prophets, who predict the demise of carbon-based life forms as the best suited 'abode' for intelligence on this planet. Oddly, the usually hostile philosophies of Platonism and Neo-Darwinism converge in a futurism that harbours an aversion to the messiness of the lived body. Nature, the 'blind watchmaker' to use Richard Dawkin's phrase, may in its *bricollage*, see fit to lay aside the body at some point in the process of its contraption building, especially if this nature finds itself (in its serendipity) sliding or pulled, into a final black hole of the virtual. Must the body of the painter likewise await this catastrophe?

Painting is a spectacle of something, only by being a 'spectacle of nothing'.[16]

Critics of ocularcentrism are hopelessly essentialist in their interrogation of various 'scopic regimes', spectacles, world-pictures, and the like. These 'regimes of the gaze' are picture postcards floating on a sea of indeterminacy. They may be beneficially examined as local 'world-pictures' but are of little use when confronting the visual in its radical openness. Life has produced a dream state in the form of human consciousness. The biological organism is *oneirotropic*. It grows towards the dream. The hypertrophy of the optical drive, as an ontogenetic development within evolutionary time, might suggest the dynamic that powers the upsurge of virtual in the midst of its going who knows where? The equipmentalisation of the optical drive casts forth the body into the virtual with the projection of the body as ray, moving from the gene to transitional points of concentration (gene-eye-virtual reality goggles, etc). As the body proper becomes increasingly deployed within its prosthetic extensions, the technophiliac fantasy of a final dispersion of the physical substrate within the realm of the virtual becomes more immanent. The virtual body would become more and more dominant, as if the body proper were in fact teleologically encoded to dissipate, liquefy, and evaporate, leaving the virtual body to continue unencumbered as pure ray.

Cultural ideograms fail; world pictures become exhausted. An ethics of the channel changer will eventually deal with modes of being in the world. Just as the real depletes itself in pursuit of the virtual on the level of the individual, so it does also in the multiplicity of bodies to form a vast social depletion. The mass of the social, or its dreaming substrate, is largely conscious of itself within the virtual, and resents the encumbrance of its material link. The sacrifice of the body for its double, its image, will be reenacted on the plane of the social, with possibly catastrophic results.

History is a Bacchanalia. One must move along in the

FROM ABOVE: Big Fall, *1984, oil and acrylic on canvas, 15.2 x 27.9cm;* Apocatastasis (Naples, Italy), *1995, 63.5 x 142.2cm*

Dionysian procession, or suffer the wrath of its mad God. Plotinus describes being as a dereliction, a wandering. Desire is reified within the trajectory of its own dereliction. This deflection, spawning as its mirror-world an allegorical labyrinth of would-be or false desire, is the 'image' of the virtual. For desire, the virtual must be made real. Only then will an Apocatastasis or reconciliation of the virtual and real, form and matter be achieved.

Whether the bodies of painters are arrayed on one line of the skirmish or the other is still open to question. More than likely they will remain double agents, and continue to surreptitiously cross the lines of battle, forever plotting to defer any final outcome for the love of the thing.

Notes

1 Gilles Deleuze, *Cinema 2: The Time-Image*, Hugh Tomilson and Robert Galeta (trans), The University of Minnesota Press,1989, p172.

2 On the faciality of the body see Gilles Deleuze and Felix Guattari, *A Thousand Plateaus: Capialism and Schizophrenia*, Brian Massumi (trans), The University of Minnesota Press, 1987, p170: 'Now the face has a correlate of great importance: the landscape, which is not just a milieu but a de-territorialized world'. Also, 'Painting . . . position[s] a landscape as a face, treating one like the other', *ibid*, p172.

3 The Schreber Case: in *The Memoirs of My Nervous Illness*, Daniel Paul Schreber presents an astonishingly lucid report of a psychosis described from within. The Schreber Case has been subjected to analysis by Freud, Lacan, Niederland, Deleuze and Guattari and many others. His identification of nerves with divine rays forms part of a dramatic cosmology focused within and around his body. This, and his description of the psychic evisceration to which his body (Deleuze and Guattari's Body without Organs) was subjected, provided me with useful terminology. *See*, Daniel Paul Schreber, *Memoirs of my Nervous Illness* (1903), I Macalpine & RA Hunter (trans & ed), Dawson, London, 1955. (Reissued with an introduction by SM Weber by Harvard University Press, 1988.)

4 Edmund Husserl, *Ideas: General Introduction to Pure Phenomenology*, WR Boyce Gibson (trans), Collier Books, New York, 1962, p314 (author's italicisation). The German original, *Ideen au einer reinen Phanomenologie und phanomenologischen Philosophie*, was published in 1913.

5 Jacques Derrida, translation and introduction to Edmund Husserl, *L'Origine de la Geometrie*, Presses Universitaires de France, Paris, 1962. English Translation: *Edmund Husserl's Origin of Geometry: An Introduction*, John P Leavey, Nicolas Hays, New York,1977, p85.

6 Ancient optics and their place in the history of visuality were considered in a series of lectures given by Ivan Illich for the Science, Technology and Society Program at the Pennsylvania State University in the autumn semesters of 1994 and 1995. Reference can be made to 'Guarding the Eye in the Age of the Show, Workings Papers No 4', *Science, Technology and Society Studies*, University Park, Pennsylvania, August 1994; Barbara Duden, Ivan Illich, and Mother Jerome, OSB, Lee Hoinacki (ed), 'The Scopic Past and the Ethics of the Gaze , Workings Papers No 6', *Science, Technology and Society Studies*, November 1995.

7 *See* Gérard Simon, 'Behind the Mirror', *Graduate Faculty Philosophy Journal*, Vol 12, Nos 1/2, The New School for Social Research, New York, p313.

8 On Proclus' cyclic theory of causation (Remaining, Procession, and Reversion) see Stephen E Gersh, *ΚΙΝΗΣΙΣ ΑΚΙΝΗΤΟΣ: A Study of Spiritual Motion in the Philosophy of Proclus*, EJ Brill, Leiden, 1973. Also SE Gersh, *From Iamlichus to Eriugena: An Investigation of the Prehistory and Evolution of the Pseudo-Dionysian Tradition*, EJ Brill, Leiden, 1978.

9 On the metaphorics of light in early Christian Neo-Platonism *see* Paul Rorem, *Biblical and Liturgical Symbols within the Pseudo-Dionysian Synthesis,* Paulist Press, New York, 1984: 'The metaphor of physical light is used to express the goal of elevation . . . and the final ascent to the ultimately blinding light of perfect darkness.' p113. 'Human minds are raised up to the "ray" which enlightens them.' From the 'Ecclesiastical Hierarchy', *Pseudo-Dionysus the Areopagite*, Paul Rorem (trans), Paulist Press, New York, 1987, p113. 'However, this divine ray can enlighten us only by being upliftingly concealed in a variety of sacred veils which the providence of the Father adapts to our nature as human beings', (Celestial Hierarchy), *ibid*, p65.

10 David Michael Levin, *The Opening of Vision: Nihilism and the Postmodern Situation*, Routledge, New York,1988, p508.

11 The anti-ocular in recent theory has been helpfully recounted by Martin Jay in *Downcast Eyes: The Denigration of Vision in Twentieth-Century French Thought*, University of California Press, Berkeley, 1993. Also of interest are Jay's comments on the 'monocular': 'Significantly, that eye was singular, rather than the two eyes of normal binocular vision. It was conceived as a lone eye looking through a peep hole at the scene in front of it. Such an eye was, moreover, understood to be static, unblinking, and fixated, rather than dynamic, moving with what later scientists would call 'saccadic' jumps from one focal point to another'. For more on the topic, see Martin Jay, 'Scopic Regimes of Modernity' *Vision and Visuality*, Hal Foster (ed), Bay Press, Seattle, 1988. My interest in this issue may in part stem from the fact that I have had monocular vision from birth. In actuality, the eye of monocular vision moves in pronouncedly rapid, saccadic jerks to compensate for the loss of stereometric depth cues. It is worth mentioning that rapid eye movement, or REM, is widely known to occur during dream sequences. More recently, research has been done regarding increased rapid eye movements in patients considered to be schizophrenic. (RY)

12 Martin Heidegger, 'The Turning', *The Question Concerning Technology and other Essays*, W Lovitt (ed), Harper and Row, New York, 1977, p38.

13 Plotinus: 'Matter's need is never met. [Matter is] . . . something abandoned . . . a thing dragged toward every shape and property and appearing to follow', Ennead III. 6, *Plotinus: The Enneads*, Stephen MacKenna (trans), John Dillon (ed), Penguin, London, 1991, p207. Also: '[The Soul] . . . in its audacity, its Tolma . . . penetrates to this sphere in a voluntary plunge . . . [I]t is under compulsion to participate in the sense realm...it reaches downward to the level of sensation . . . [This] "solice by flight" of Heraclitus [is] . . . a wandering away . . . a voluntary descent which is also involuntary'. 'Ennead IV. 8', *ibid*, p339-40.

14 Martin Jay, *Scopic Regimes of Modernity*, p27.

15 *See* Bynum, Caroline Walker, *The Resurrection of the Body in Western Christianity, 200-1336*. Columbia University Press, New York, 1995.

16 Maurice Merleau Ponty, *Phenomenology of Perception*, Colin Smith (trans), Routeledge and Kegan Paul, London, 1962, p141.

THOUGHT IS PHYSICAL

The whitewashed tree or post that momentarily startles us in a dark country lane takes on the guise that expectancy gives it. The mental predisposition here becomes the dominant factor, and the timid see as ghosts what their more sturdy companions recognize as whitewashed posts. Such experiences we ascribe to the action of suggestion and imagination—the cloud "that's almost in shape like a camel," or "like a weasel,"or "like a whale." But throughout our visual experiences there runs this double strain, now mainly outward and now mainly inward, from the simplest excitements of the retina up to the realms where fancy soars free from the confines of sense, and the objective finds its occupation gone.

—Jastrow, *Fact and Fable in Psychology*

THE STATE OF THE PROJECTION

Who is in position to propose?

Not so long ago the projection was revamped to make it more psychological. As if doctors could re-rig the old archaic lines. Projections exchanged their vanishing points(Alberti) for family triangles(Lacan), slicker geometries of loss and drive. Nobody much saw red. Everybody supposedly drove off to lack, that now vanished point.

Wasn't it the blues?

Color made no difference to the duck-rabbit,

the one Jastrow saw was dark and hairy, Wittgenstein's was white, both showed what they had to show, which is to say themselves. But neither quacked or multiplied because neither was either one. You two. No one moving, hunting, driving. Who was moved? What lacked? Time now to reproject and take the animal somewhere else, abandon the games not won. Forget the tear that was a tear. Look the little faces in the eye. Tuck them in. Hair-feathers, appendages, behaviors slip off at night, mere characteristic, sheath. Let the eye close, leaving too, lights out, all sleep, no point. Doubles are no longer the beginning and the end of it. There are still deeper, winter sleeps.

What happens when the rabbit dies?

Then duck?

It passed.

Read blew.

I knew them once as primaries.

texts **m. nesbit**
images **d.turner**

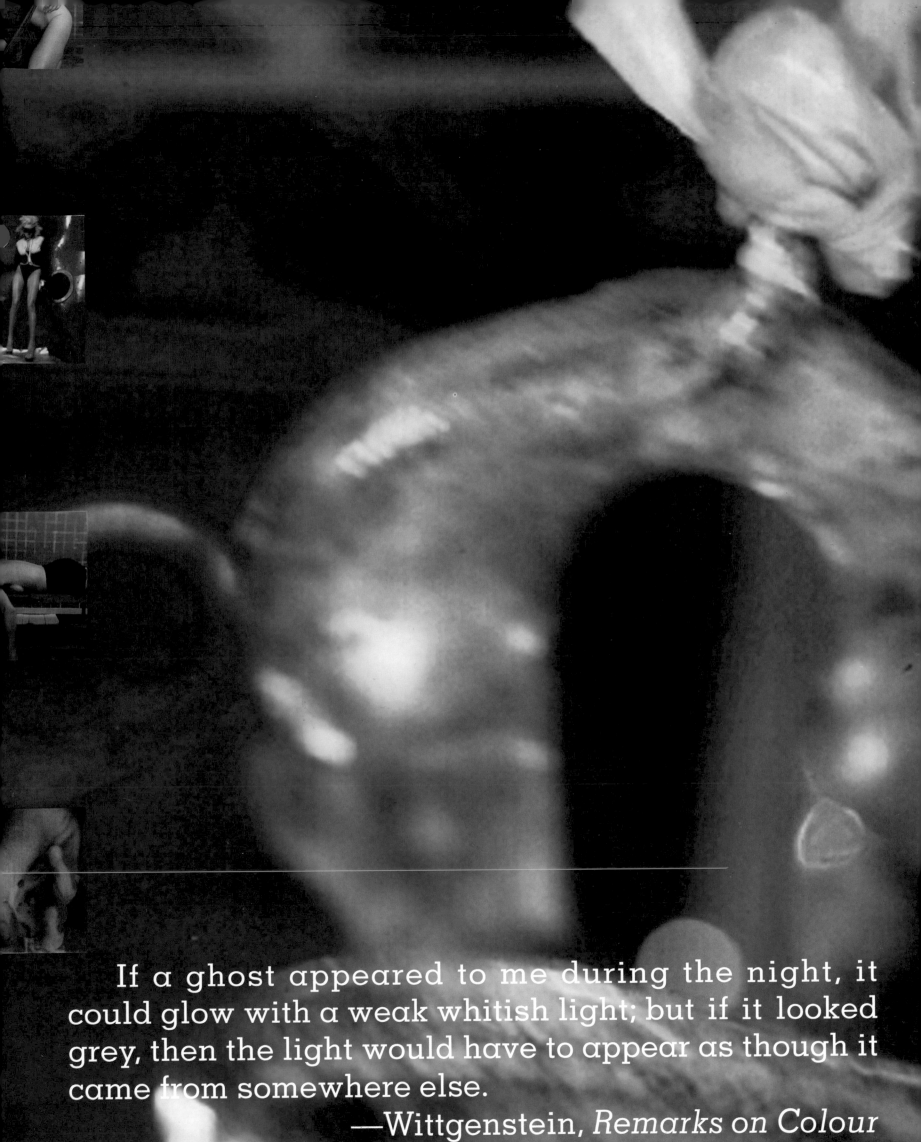

If a ghost appeared to me during the night, it could glow with a weak whitish light; but if it looked grey, then the light would have to appear as though it came from somewhere else.
—Wittgenstein, *Remarks on Colour*

FROM ABOVE: William Blair Bruce, Summer Night Effect in Sweden at 2am when it is neither day nor night, *oil on canvas, 136 x 250cm; Robert Longo,* Untitled, *(from the* Johnny *paintings), 1994, acrylic on canvas, 152.4 x 152.4cm*

FOILED AGAIN

Ihor Holubizky

Jack Burnham launched a curatorial salvo with the *Software* exhibition at the Jewish Museum in 1970. His vision was a movement away from art-making and objects, the craft aesthetic, and what he called the 'mental cues' of art history:

> Most of Software is anionic; its images are usually secondary or instructional while its information often takes the form of printed materials.

Another proposition, by Theodor H Nelson, the technical adviser for *Software,* added to the *McLuhanesque* assault; 'our bodies are hardware, our behaviour software'. Burnham, however, skirts the term Artificial Intelligence (AI) in dealing with the elusive connection between science, technology and art. AI may ultimately come to rest where it began, in science and research, as a theoretical model to impart intelligent processes to machines by a communication link to the human operators, not to turn the machine into a sentient being. What has come to pass in cultural models is the latter, the monster creations we all fear – a line stretching from Frankenstein, Robby the Robot, to Dr Noonian Soong's twin androids of *Star Trek: TNG*, Lore and Data. Each embodies something beyond verification: that which separates us from lower order species; that which allows us to hold and consider abstract ideas. But there is a need to believe in things beyond our understanding. Call this the mental grist to the mill wheel of the artificial world, in contrast to the biochemical condition of the natural world for survival and propagation of the species. There are unavoidable problems with AI application experiments. Frankenstein lacked social skills, the ability to verbalise and conduct himself with commonsense survival. Robby the Robot – although a multilinguist with superhuman strength and skills – was hampered by appearance, as much as Mr F, his grunting predecessor. Robby's espresso machine outfit could only have been taken seriously in a night club. Data poses another problem as the ultimate achievement, a sentient being proven in legal court, in one episode of *Star Trek: TNG*. His flaw was wanting to be flawed, to be human, to go night clubbing. Such a wish can be said to be a lack of intelligence. Of 'The Four', only Data is known to have taken brush to canvas.

Art has some connection as an impractical sign. Painting crosses the court constantly – to be one thing and then another, purposeful and self-determining. The completed work of art is sent out into the world to create mayhem. The foul line – between genre and modernism, abstraction and representation – is not drawn so simply. After a century of modernism, image-making still remains at the threshold, with abstraction. But if the latter

commands the higher spiritual plane and demands intelligence to decode and appreciate, the flip side is the incantation, 'this is what it is and nothing more'. Dumb and dumber.

The flaw of *Software* was that future-seeking could not assure the creation of compelling art, no matter how the definition of art is changed or denied to accommodate the future. One of the highlights was *Seek,* 1969-70, developed by the Architecture Machine Group from MIT. This installation-cum-demonstration incorporated an elementary prosthesis guided by a 'blind and handless' computer. The prosthesis, a sardonic reprise of Michelangelo's *The Creation of Adam*, continually altered the closed environment inhabited by a small colony of gerbils, by rearranging toy blocks – adapting as the gerbils adapted to changing conditions. One of the live crew for *Seek* was Nicholas Negroponte, the Col Saunders of cyberspace – touting 11 herbs and spices in the secret recipe. The Group's statement, 'if computers are to be our friends they must understand our metaphors', was countered by the catalogue cover, stating in appropriate tabloid form: 'Gerbils match wits with computer-built environment'. The grand experiment of *Seek* overlooked the gerbils, who were unlikely to befriend prosthesis, computer, or MIT.

Painting is the last place one expects to witness the match of present-future wits, but painting may still hold a key to meaningful information between ideas, creator and viewer. Painting can present a believable representation of the world, natural and artificial. It can also fast track and eliminate all representation . . . and in doing so, claim the very same. The 'nothing more than what we see' is, therefore, subject to terms and conditions of lived experience and the metaphysical.

Two paintings, at opposite ends of the century, offer a comparative dialogue and the meeting of intelligences; William Blair Bruce's *Summer Night Effect in Sweden at 2 am when it is neither day nor night* [1], and a Robert Longo untitled *Johnny* painting from 1994. Bruce – a Canadian, Hamilton-born artist – lived and worked in Europe in the last two decades of the 19th century. Some have referred to him as a dabbler – romantic realism, post-impressionism, society portraiture, and Baltic seascapes done in Turnerisms. *Summer Night Effect . . .* is a mystery, as much as the mystery of its title – a salon-scaled painting of a family group – a splendour in the grass in the tradition of Manet's *Déjeuner sur l'Herbe* (1863). There are obvious distinctions. Bruce's figures are nude, caught in an unexplainable family/social ritual; a scene revealed by the painter leading the viewer. Answers to 'why be nude at 2am in Sweden?' and 'what exactly is the summer night effect?' may be all the more difficult because this painting was probably unfinished. Taken at interrupted face value, it could be a foray into Symbolism, but judging by Bruce's 'finished' work, consistent resolution cannot be assumed. Bruce could, as in *The Happy Meeting* (1893), create a believable pastiche with vastly different types of painting – the mimetic to the impressionistic. Bruce concocted a highly organised and wholly fictitious moment – the scene of a man, woman and dog on a country bridge – in the guise of reportage, where the pastoral, bucolic mood converges with the modern world. A stream of smoke is visible in the background, its source unseen. It could be the result of a field fire, or the trail from a passing train. We may be looking at a fabulation in *Summer Night Effect* . . . but we are also looking at the ground of paint itself and the weave of the canvas telegraphing through the paint like a binary code. The figures appear blurred, in motion, with foliage dissolving in an effect of light and colour. Nothing comes clearly into view – a vision expressed as the effect of a matter transporter device, beaming up or beaming down.

Robert Longo's *Johnny* painting appears remote from Blair Bruce's world – painting which defies and admires; positing a cloaked meaning. One critical distinction is that Bruce was trained to be a painter while Longo admits to being a creature-creation of cultural journalism, unsure of where he stands; 'It seemed I was too smart for the pop world and too pop for the art world'.[2] Longo publically stated that the art world 'made' him and has to deal with him and, presumably, with his mayhem.[3] At face value, Longo's painting is unremarkable – a wash across a lazy gesture. A watered-down Morris Louis via Paul Jenkins; a 1990s wannabe of the 1960s New York School? This is the very thing which can infuriate painters and leave Longo's admirers puzzled. After all, where is the intelligence in this artifice? By intent or happy meeting, Longo has left an attitudinal creation at the doorstep of a discourse and history, the artificial condition consistent with his career. The *Johnny* paintings are so guileless as to make all like painting, which takes its position with solemn grace, suspect. But in a museum collection, Longo's painting is an agent provocateur, a virus in the storage banks of painting, no less intelligent   just ugly. The notion of ugly invokes the age-old gambit of value judgement and aesthetics, now applied to a cultural milieu which rebels against such categorisation, but fosters another form of gamesmanship.

In Longo's 1995 feature film *Johnny Mnemonic,* the main character known only as Johnny, is a data courier with faulty hardware – his body a host to a lethal parasite. Longo would have us believe that the *Johnny* paintings done during the filming are an addendum relating to the subtext of a film which carries a familiar plot – a variant on *The Man in the White Suit* (Alexander Mackendrick, 1951), or *The Man Who Knew Too Much* (Alfred Hitchcock, 1956). Burnham discounted seeing for knowing, but in Johnny's quest for freedom, he dons a visor ('blind I tell you, he's blind!'), touching and 'seeking' his way with prosthetic data gloves. He may be connected to software systems – out of body – but reacts to images, much as McLuhan connected his mid-century view of *The Mechanical Bride* (1951) to reading the subtext of advertising . . . before New York Pop and before Richard Hamilton's 1956 collage, *Just what is it that makes today's homes so different, so appealing?* Hamilton's collage can be wound back to Blair Bruce as a body hammer of glamour, vulgarity, kitsch, and ego which has an 'effect' – a celestial sky, Hamilton's Sistine Chapel. Blair Bruce's 'seeing', and what we don't see, requires knowing . . . and believing.

Johnny, in contrast to the Bruce mystery, does have an access code, three random images from a sci-fi cartoon on Japanese television. It could have easily been three stills from *Wheel of Fortune*, but that would be irony, and irony has no place in Johnny's world – a slugfest of the obvious. The frozen cartoon figures – evoking the frozen gesture of Longo's 1979-1982 drawings, *Men in the Cities* (women too) – come to play in cyberspace, Johnny's dream/nightmare space . . . when it is neither day nor night. They are simple keys to complex information, a cure for a modern affliction. In the film's climax, as Johnny is set to have the data downloaded, the rebel J-Bone, played by ganster rap performer Ice-T, tells the world to set its VCRs to record, as if it were another TV show.

There is no way to reconcile Bruce and Longo, to place them on a level playing field in a contemporary discourse, but they do bracket a similar agenda for painting: artificiality in the pursuit of intelligence. The paintings may also come together in the potential of being mapped onto each other. Longo's painting gestures can be read as Bruce's effect of the summer night. Johnny can be transported to Sweden, sitting butt-naked, a target, desiring nothing more than a clean shirt. If the desire for clothing cannot be determined by Bruce's subjects, Ice-T lays it on the line; 'we'll undress by the light of the moon. Lay down and I'll caress that butt'.[4] In the seemingly slow medium of painting – the antithesis to the hyperspeed world – there is the sensorineural. It is the quality ascribed to AI – layers of information which can be penetrated but hold and form a coherent language. Cognition – inspiration – requires silence. Painting, resting in a soundproof chamber, participates in the story and returns us to the oral tradition. It leads us to some understanding of nature – what may lie on the surface and below the surface without ever having been there.

Notes

1 Undated, but likely painted after 1900 and before 1906, the year of Bruce's death: The alternative title is *The Hawthorns*.

2 *The Globe and Mail* (Toronto), 17 September 1994.

3 *Artnews*, October 1989, p149.

4 Ice-T, 'Girls L.G.B.N.A.F.', *Power*, Sire Records, 1988.

Dina Meyer (Jane) and Keanu Reeves (Johnny) in director Robert Longo's Johnny Mnemonic, *1995, black and white still*

PAINTING THEORY MACHINES

Warren Sack

Spectators[1] of ten years ago spun a series of writings around art work variously termed 'simulationist', 'neo-geo', and 'neo-futurist'. Reception of the 'simulationist' work – a reception which drew its philosophical strength from Jean Baudrillard's theory of the *simulacrum*[2] – engendered a comparison between, for instance, paintings and technoscientific instruments of simulation (eg, computer programs and techniques of cloning and gene manipulation). As a software designer I was intrigued by this theoretical convergence of painting analysis and high technology since it offered a possible means of rethinking digital artefacts through the problems of painting and vice versa. Yet, the past decade has revealed a variety of weaknesses in strategies that employ Baudrillard's simulacrum as a map of reception. Moreover, even ten years ago, many were sceptical of a comparison or 'engagement' between high technology and traditional high art. Hal Foster voiced his scepticism about 'simulationist' painting: can this work seriously engage issues of a technoscientific, post-industrial society in a medium, like painting, based in preindustrial craft?[3] More recently, some spectators have turned away from Baudrillard to the writings of philosophers Gilles Deleuze and Félix Guattari to theorise the work of a group of artists, often related but different to the 'simulationists' of the mid-80s. For example, several authors in a recent issue of the *Journal of Philosophy and the Visual Arts* discussed painting with the help of a Deleuzean-Guattarian lexicon.[4] I believe that this shift in theoretics facilitates a means of viewing painting *not* as equivalent to the artefacts and processes of high technology but as distinctly different to the kinds of work that scientists and engineers currently engage in:

> For their part, the paradigms of techno-science place the emphasis on an objectified world of relations and functions, systematically bracketing out subjective affects, such that the finite, the delimited and coordinatable, always takes precedence over the infinite and its virtual references. With art, on the contrary, the finite quality of the sensible material becomes a support for the production of affects and percepts which tend to become more and more decentred with respect to preformed structures and coordinates. Marcel Duchamp declared: 'art is a road which leads towards regions which are not governed by time and space'.[5]

In the sentences quoted above, Guattari emphasises differences between techno-science and art. Moreover, elsewhere, Guattari articulates differences between his own work and the work of techno-science: 'My perspective involves shifting the human and social sciences from scientific paradigms towards ethico-aesthetic paradigms.'[6] I see an interesting tension between this emphasis on the *divergence* of the arts, sciences, and Deleuze and Guattari's own work, and the *convergences* that have been emphasised by Deleuze and some translators and scholars of Deleuze and Guattari.

Various writers have noted a convergence between Deleuze's work and the scientific theories of complexity and chaos (developed in fields like physics and computer science). Brian Massumi, the English-language translator of Deleuze and Guattari's book *Thousand Plateaus*, said the following in a recent article:

> [Gilles Deleuze's] work . . . could profitably be read together with recent theories of complexity and chaos. It is a question of *emergence*, which is precisely the focus of the various science-derived theories which converge around the notion of self-organisation (the spontaneous production of a level of reality having its own rules of formation and order of connection).[7]

Manuel De Landa, in his book *War in the Age of Intelligent Machines* meticulously expounds on the ways in which Deleuze's work intersects with theories of complexity, chaos and self-organisation.[8] Indeed, Deleuze emphasises his own mathematical and scientific 'borrowings' in such work as Chapter 15 of his book *Logic of Sense*.[9]

In the following essay I will play with these tensions of divergence and convergence which run through Deleuze and Guattari's work. I am interested in investigating how the different theoretical machines and simulacra of Baudrillard and Deleuze and Guattari have been shaped into instruments of reception to allow a viewer to see parallels and differences between the artefacts of painting and the artefacts of science and technology. I understand various uses of Baudrillard's theories as felicitous to a 'reading' of painting which emphasises its convergence with the products of science and technology. I use the theories of Deleuze and Guattari to explain a set of divergences that I see separating computer science and a certain kind of

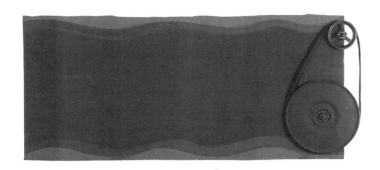

Moira Dryer, The Perpetual Painting, *1988, case in lacquer on found auto parts, wood, 91.4 x 210.8 x 10.2cm*

contemporary painting. Actually, it is more precise to say that I use painting to describe differences I see between the machines of Deleuze and Guattari and the machines of the computational sciences.

As an expository device I will rely on mathematician Alan Turing's theory of machines to stand-in for all computer science. Alan Turing was the 'inventor' of computers and of artificial intelligence. In 1936, Turing wrote a technical paper entitled 'On Computable Numbers, with an Application to the *Entscheidungsproblem*'.[10] Turing's paper provided the 'blueprint' for the developers of the first electronic computers. It continues to be a seminal paper for all computer scientists because, in his paper, Turing mathematically demonstrated what can imprecisely be understood as the assertion that it is impossible to build a computer more powerful than a Turing machine; ie, the theoretical apparatus called a Turing machine is capable of 'simulating' all possible computers. Consequently, it is generally believed that to understand the limitations of computers in general, one need only investigate the specific limitations of Turing machines.

Of course this methodology is not always employed by theorists of computation because they have identified a variety of other formalisms which are 'equivalent' to Turing machines. However, it does mean that any precise argument demonstrating the limitations of a Turing machine could, potentially, have far-reaching implications for all computational media. Alan Turing is also considered to be the 'father' of the field of artificial intelligence due to another article published in 1950 entitled 'Computing Machinery and Intelligence'.[11] Thus, it is often considered worthwhile, even today, for computer scientists to re-examine Turing's original work.

In this essay I return to Turing's original papers to compare Turing machines with the kinds of 'desiring machines' that some painters are said to produce around Deleuze and Guattari's theories. I outline a set of irreconcilable differences, or *differends* (in philosopher Jean-François Lyotard's terms[12]) which exist between Turing machines and those of Deleuze and Guattari. I think these *differends* can be seen or 'read' in certain forms of contemporary painting. I understand this essay as an effort to create for myself (and possibly others) a means of viewing painting as divergent from the projects of techno-science and yet, simultaneously, involved in an 'engagement' with techno-science; an 'engagement' which involves the use of art as a way of seeing possible alternatives to existing science and technology.

The *differends* that I identify are analogous to well-known formal problems that painters have been addressing for centuries. I can list them here: (1) Grids: while Turing machines are founded upon a strict attention to the 'grid', 'desiring machines' are formulated in a smooth, unstriated space which can break the 'grid'; (2) Signs: Turing machines assume a finite, fixed 'alphabet,' while 'desiring machines' and the painting which produces them is often concerned with the production of new signs, new marks, perhaps infinitesimally – yet significantly – different from the 'alphabets' of other painting or (post)industrial processes; and, (3) Details: Turing's definitions assume that one will ignore 'inconvenient' or 'unprofitable' details, while it is never *a priori* obvious for the functioning of a 'desiring machine' which details are significant and which are to be ignored. The rest of this essay can be read as an expansion of these 'formal' details of painting which, I believe, can lead to an investigation of ethical considerations like these: for whom is a particular detail unimportant? Who has the will and the power to produce a new sign? How are spatial divisions negotiated?

Turing Machines

It is an extended process of enculturation to arrive at the point where one believes that a Turing machine is 'universal'. Roughly speaking, this belief is tantamount to believing that anything a person can do, in a systematic manner, with a surface of inscription and a stylus, one can get a computer to do or at least to 'simulate'. The full blown belief that engenders one to equate mental states to the coded states of Turing's finite discrete state machines requires that one be dragged through the complexities of how David Hilbert, in 1928, challenged the mathematics community to prove mathematics *complete*, *consistent* and *decidable* and how, in response, Kurt Gödel showed mathematics to be *incomplete* and *inconsistent* and how Alan Turing and Alonzo Church showed it to be *undecidable*.

The ideological state apparatus that drags one through this quite stunning and impressive controversy is the school, or

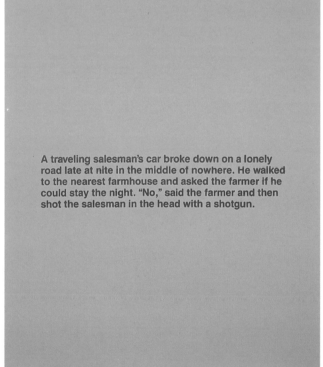

A traveling salesman's car broke down on a lonely road late at nite in the middle of nowhere. He walked to the nearest farmhouse and asked the farmer if he could stay the night. "No," said the farmer and then shot the salesman in the head with a shotgun.

FROM ABOVE: Richard Prince, Almost Grown, *1989, fibreglass, wood, oil and enamel, 158.1 x 132.1 x 8.9cm, (photo, Larry Lame); Richard Prince,* Untitled (Joke), *1988, acrylic and silkscreen on canvas, 142.2 x 121.9cm*

rather the university, as it acts upon computer science undergraduates. Turing's and Gödel's proofs[13] both rely on techniques of enumeration and diagonalisation invented by mathematician Georg Cantor over a century after Kant outlined his theory of the sublime. Kant's mathematical sublime is a cognitive state and crucially relies upon a subject's contemplation of enumeration and infinity.[14] However, as the neo-Kantian Jean-François Lyotard points out, Kant's 'mathematical sublime' is not just one kind of sublime among many, it is just one way of describing the sublime.[15] I do not know of a better way to describe Gödel's and Turing's preoccupation with enumeration which led them to the sweet-sorrow, the pleasure-pain,[16] of making huge advances in the field of mathematics while, at the same time, undermining basic tenants of the discipline. Specifically, Turing's handling of decidability, Hilbert's *Entscheidungsproblem*, show a way in which, with finite means and an innumerable infinity of steps, one can create an 'unsolvable problem'. This, for the mathematics community, was the phenomenon created by an inward, reflexive turn – an application of the rules of mathematics to the behaviour of mathematicians – that led to a giant crack, leak, threatening to suck mathematics into the formless void of the 'outside', the unknowable, the *noumena*.

Baudrillard and the Simulationists

It is uncanny, in the Freudian sense, to see how the problems of computational incompleteness, inconsistency and undecidability are repressed in the everyday thinking of certain computer scientists and others who marvel at the capabilities and ubiquitousness of contemporary computational media, like 'virtual reality' and the Internet. One hears over and over how practically anything – sex, flight, reasoning – can be 'simulated'. Indeed, it seems to me that this is the bandwagon that Jean Baudrillard climbed on-board with the writing of his essay 'Simulacra and Simulations'. Baudrillard tells us – as Borges and the International Situationist, Guy Debord, did earlier[17] – that now the 'map precedes the territory':[18]

> the cartographer's mad project of an ideal coextensivity between the map and the territory, disappears with simulation, whose operation is nuclear and genetic . . . genetic miniaturisation is the dimension of simulation. The real is produced from miniaturised units, from matrices, memory banks and command models – and with these it can reproduce an indefinite number of times.[19]

Baudrillard's essay excited a lot of interest within the circles of various painters and sculptures. It has been used, for example, to describe the pictures of the 'Pictures' show organised by Douglas Crimp for Artists Space in New York[20] and the art of the Metro Pictures Gallery artists of the late-70s and early-80s.[21] Thereafter, Baudrillard's 'simulacra' underwrote the escape from East Village neo-expressionism by Peter Halley and other 'neo-geo', 'simulationist', 'neo-futurist' artists.[22] Enigmatically though it appears that these artists did not really believe in the powers of digital simulation the way, for example, the Russian Constructivists or the Italian Futurists subscribed to the age of industrial machinations earlier in the century. A technophilia, on the order of the Constructivists, precipitated a renunciation of painting in favour of the *métiers* of industrial design, engineering and documentary photography.[23] Apparently, Baudrillard did not manage to even convince himself of the powers of digital simulation for, if he had, where now are the painters-turned-computer-programmers, the philosophers-turned-software-engineers?

Actually, in 1996, we all know the answer to this question: these former painters and philosophers are now in 'digital multimedia', an industry based upon a misunderstanding of Marshall McLuhan, even as its headlight publication, *Wired*, claims McLuhan on its masthead as 'patron saint' of the magazine. McLuhan, in *Understanding Media*, claims that every new medium institutes new ratios between our senses.[24] He does not say that new media are replacements for older media. Instead, his idea is that the introduction of new media serve as 'extensions' to ourselves and, simultaneously, they 'amputate' various capacities of subjectivity. Multimedia enthusiasts often believe in 'convergence' of the media and that 'bits are bits' such that any media can be translated into, and thus replaced by, digital media. Belief in the idea that everything can be translated into one (digital, computational) substrate – rather than being a challenge to Clement Greenberg's monomedia mania[25] – is actually an 'extension' of Greenberg's work. Greenberg's belief in a vantage point from which any artefact can be assigned its proper medium, has its analogue in multimedia's subscription to the computer as the 'universal machine' that can handle any new medium (eg video) simply through the addition of a new *codec* (compression/decompression algorithm) and display peripheral (eg, a colour screen or three-dimensional printer).

Multimedia personnel aside (as a member of the MIT Media Laboratory, perhaps I need to step aside at this point too), I want to concentrate on those artists and philosophers who heard Baudrillard's message, but who did not submit to the technophilia implicit in his essay. Instead, these painters continued to paint, the sculptors to sculpt, and the philosophers to write. In 1986, at the Boston Institute for Contemporary Art *Endgame* show,[26] Baudrillard's simulacra were seen as an escape from the essentialising, minimalisations inflicted on abstract painting and sculpture by the previous generations of conceptual and abstract artists. The 'way out' was a refusal of the 'real' for the 'not-real,' the 'simulacrum'.

At the level of praxis, it was clear at the time – in the mid-80s – that the artists understood Baudrillard's message in so far as, if 'everything is now just simulacrum', there is no need to give up painting for computer programming because both are equally implicated in the processes of simulation. However, the rationale for this praxis stumbled in Baudrillard's post-Marxist dialectics; specifically, in his implicit use of the opposition of the 'real' to the 'not-real'. Of course the critics caught on to this lingering dialectics immediately and teased the Marx out, often through Freud, in the figure of the fetish. To speak of, for example, Jeff Koons' fascination with consumer items as fetish objects seemed to make even good vernacular sense as one, for instance, talks of a 'fetish' in the sense of an unhealthy obsession. Hal Foster's essay in the *Endgame* catalogue is a wonderful exhibit of a Freudian/Marxist dialectical analysis in action.[27] Ultimately though, the Baudrillardian rationale implodes in its lingering dialectics since, if everything is simulacrum, then what is this 'thing' (the Kantian *ding-an-sich*, thing-in-itself) that the fetish of simulacrum is replacing? A cathectic resolution to this tension was lurking in the English-speaking world in a translation of a non-dialectical, French articulation of the simulacrum cited in another article by Hal Foster on the 'simulationists':[28] Rosalind Krauss' translation of Gilles Deleuze's 'Plato and the Simulacrum'.[29]

Deleuze and the Simulacrum

In his 1986 article for *Art in America*, 'Signs Taken for Wonders',[30] Foster does not tease out the technical details which separate Baudrillard's simulacra from Deleuze's. I think though that tracing through Deleuze's distinctions both gives one another understanding of what it could mean for everything to be a simulacrum without recourse to the problematic, dichotomy of real/not-real, and; allows one to grope through the vast, dark space which separates dialectics (eg, Hegelian) from non-dialectics (eg, the Nietzschean Eternal Return).

John Rajchman, in a recent article on painting and abstraction (entitled 'Another View of Abstraction')[31] distinguishes Deleuze's simulacra from Baudrillard's like this:

> one can argue that 'post-modernist' art remains, as it were, haunted by the spirit of the abstract painting; it only repeats this game as farce, through quotation, parody, irony, alternating between mania and melancholia. Indeed the very idea of 'appropriation', and of what Baudrillard called the 'simulacrum', is fully impregnated with the tradition of melancholy and panicked reaction to Loss or Absence; in this respect it is quite unlike the idea of the simulacrum that a forgetful Baudrillard had 'appropriated' from Deleuze, which involves not a loss but an *intensification* of the real, linked to a condition of things prior to Forms.[32]

Unlike Rajchman, I am not a philosopher and so I hope I do not damage his explanation by re-reading Deleuze's 'Plato and the Simulacrum'[33] and its repetitions (which can be found embedded in Deleuze's books *Difference and Repetition*[34] and *Logic of Sense*)[35] in order to elaborate how Deleuze's simulacrum refuses a dialectical interpretation. Firstly, Deleuze makes a distinction between the dialectics of Hegel and Plato (as it is demonstrated in the *Phaedrus*, the *Statesman*, and the *Sophist*).[36] Hegel's dialectic moves from thesis to antithesis to synthesis.

Yet, at the moment of the formulation of the antithesis, the negation of the thesis, what would happen if negation is an impossibility? For Plato, the contemplation of such an impossibility never arises because negation is not the operation invoked to produce an alternative to the thesis. Instead, Plato relies upon the invocation of myth:

> Thus, the myth constructs the immanent model or the foundation test, according to which the claimants must be judged and their claim measured. It is on this condition that division pursues and achieves its goal, which is not the specification of concept but the authentication of Idea, not the determination of species but the selection of lineage.[37]

From a post-Vladimir-Propp,[38] post-Lévi-Strauss,[39] post-Algirdas-Greimas,[40] narrative vantage point, one can see that any given myth can be canonised, or idealised, as a composition of functions, actants, or roles; for instance, the roles of hero, villain and helper and their interactions; statesman, lover, or sophist; or, even some of Hegel's *dramatis personae*, like the roles of lord and bondsman. Thus, invocation of a myth allows the conceptualisation of not just one alternative (the negation), but many which are all interrelated in some narrative and functional structure. Plato then uses the mythic, narrative structure to establish an ordering on the alternatives. Last, for Plato according to Deleuze, in any such ordering of preference are the *simulacra*, roughly those *personae* who belong to other myths not selected or who belong to no myths whatsoever.[41]

Deleuze's move from here is quite clear and hinges on a question of this kind: What if there are no such myths or idealised forms? What if, instead, such myths are in continual flux and can only be seen as singularities rather than similarities to the situation at hand? This is Deleuze's scepticism which creates the possibility that all the alternatives are semblances or simulacra and no idealised ordering on the alternatives is possible.[42] This shift in focus pushes the simulacrum, the subject without place, the nomad, into the fray. Thus it is the Zarathustran figure, the voice from the wilderness, who is left, not to order but to invigorate and intensify the various forces in play.

The disorder, de-founding, *effondement*[43] from which such simulacra emerge is, in opposition to Plato's idealised Forms, a formless *a priori* that precedes everything and connects everything, much as Henri Bergson said the 'life-force,' *élan vital,* is said to flow through everything and thereby render any subject/object divisions a problem.

Desiring Machines

If I can be permitted one more dip into the deep pool of Deleuzean philosophy I will finally be in a position from which I can explain how this juncture of painting and philosophy differs from Turing machines on several crucial points. To describe this position I must first swim into the textual flows employed by Deleuze and Guattari in the *Anti-Oedipus*[44] to shape their

'abstract machines'. It is these 'abstract machines' which have been used by contemporary critics and painters alike to distinguish some of the newer abstract painting (by for example, Lydia Dona and Fabian Marcaccio) from the mid-80s Baudrillardian 'simulationist' work (of, for example, Peter Halley and Sherrie Levine).[45]

Deleuze and Guattari's machines are based upon *effondement*, an infinitude of interlinked, chaotic flows which were previous to the emergence of any sort of form in the universe. This provides a radical alternative to a Platonic formulation wherein the world is organised around a set of idealised forms. It is also an alternative to a Lacanian (or Hegelian) conception of the subject as based upon lack or need.[46] For Deleuze and Guattari subject/object divisions and all types of discrete isolations and boundaries are interruptions. It is the abstract, *desiring* machines which interrupt, break, detach and slice the continuous flux and flows.[47] Simultaneously, the machines also connect and reconnect specific flows.[48]

Desiring Machines and Turing Machines

It is now possible for me to begin to address a question posed by John Rajchman (in his essay 'Another View of Abstraction')[49] by comparing, aspect-by-aspect, Deleuze and Guattari's 'desiring machines' to computer science's 'Turing machines':

> The question of abstraction then becomes: to what sort of 'abstract machines' do Turing machines belong; with what sort of 'desiring machines' are they connected?[50]

I think Turing himself – in his 1950 article 'Computing Machinery and Intelligence'[51] which is credited as the founding article of artificial intelligence (AI) – has a response to Rajchman's question. Unfortunately, AI researchers have consistently repressed the details of Turing's proposal while, simultaneously, crediting him as the 'father of AI.' In the 1950 essay, Turing proposes a test to determine if a computer is intelligent. His test is based upon a parlour game. I will use Turing's words to describe the game and the role he thinks it could play in determining the answer to the question 'Can machines think?'

> The new form of the problem can be described in terms of a game which we call the 'imitation game.' It is played with three people, a man (A), a woman (B), and an interrogator (C) who may be of either sex. The interrogator stays in a room apart from the other two. The object of the game for the interrogator is to determine which of the other two is the man and which is the woman . . . We now ask the question, 'What will happen when a machine takes the part of [the man] A in this game?' Will the interrogator decide wrongly as often when the game is played like this as he does when the game is played between a man and a woman? These questions replace our original, 'Can machines think?'[52]

AI researchers have chosen to remember Turing's proposal, not as a variant of the 'imitation game' which involves a machine, a woman, and an interrogator, but rather, as something that they refer to as the 'Turing Test' which involves only two players: a machine and a human. Gender differences, the focus and pivotal element of Turing's 'imitation game,' have almost uniformly been ignored by AI researchers, even in their essays about the 'Turing Test.' I have made one important omission in my description of Turing's 'imitation game.' Turing intended the man, in the original game, to play the role of a woman. The point of this being that both the man and the woman are suppose to try and convince the interrogator that they are the woman. In other words, Turing's original proposal was, essentially, to build a machine to function as a man pretending to be a woman.

Such a masquerade is not only familiar to fans of Shakespearean theatre; it is also a common masquerade on the Internet where it is quite simple to 'change one's gender' by, for example, using a fictitious name or 'handle' when writing electronic mail (E-mail) messages or when participating in 'on-line' discussions. The desires which lurk behind an E-mail question from one user regarding another user's 'real' gender are constitutive of the sorts of 'desiring machines' that contemporary Turing machines and their users are connected to. I do not think it is an exaggeration to say that Turing's original essay suggests a very different kind of AI than the AI which has been developed over the past 45 years. What is even more intriguing is how this 'alternative' AI – which one can imagine could preserve the centrality of the gender issues Turing posed in his essay – would have something of interest to say about the ubiquity of cross-gender masquerades on the Internet. While I, as a software designer, hope to contribute towards the creation of such an alternative AI, right now I want to turn to what I see as the response of painting to Rajchman's question.

Baudrillard, Turing and Halley

My 'degree zero' for this discussion on painting and Turing machines will be the work of Peter Halley. In much of his work Halley uses rigid geometric forms to investigate flow charts, flow diagrams and the related codes of system analysts, computer programmers, and urban planners. I will argue that these works by Halley, done over the course of the last 15 years, illustrate a very tight coupling to the Baudrillardian and Turing – thus computational – conceptions of machinery and simulation. I will also argue – and thus their position as a 'degree zero' – that these works by Halley have very little to offer in the way of exercising Deleuze and Guattari's 'abstract machines'. I hope that by introducing Deleuze and Guattari's machines and contrasting them with Turing's, I will be able to show how various painters – often associated with Halley but working on their own conceptions of machinery and simulacra – create an alternative to the concept of Turing machines as 'universal machines'.

In writing about the 'New York Painters', Arthur C Danto

points out that 'painting-as-writing does not capture all the painters of New York today – but it does define the artists gathered here [Peter Halley, Jonathan Lasker, Philip Taaffe, Ross Bleckner], and a great many more, whose artistic agendas it helps clarify'.[53] Following Danto, and listening to Halley, one can quickly see the relationship between Halley's paintings and Turing machines, the 'writings' of computation:

Jeff Rian: Is there a logical relationship between the flowcharts and your paintings?
Peter Halley: When I was planning to include them in my Dallas show some people said that it would be too didactic to put a flowchart next to a painting to show the connections between them. But I use flowcharts that are as opaque as possible; in other words there is no specific information. In fact, they make no sense without their captions. What happened in Dallas was that viewers first looked at the flowcharts, then they looked at the paintings. I think it was a way of giving the average person information about the paintings.[54]

It is useful to remember that the 'flowcharts' Halley refers to here are not linked with Deleuze and Guattari's 'flows'. Instead, these 'flowcharts' are, essentially, an alternative notation for Turing machines. Halley usefully separates himself from a Deleuzean interpretation by saying later in the same interview 'I don't really think of myself as a schizophrenic artist in the sense of, say, Richter or Polke . . . '[55] Since Deleuze and Guattari specifically call their theoretical stance 'schizoanalysis',[56] Halley's comment seems to interrupt attempts to represent his work as Deleuzean and to encourage a reading of it as an aspect of Baudrillard's simulacra and the simulations of Turing machines.

Anyone who has seen computer microprocessors under high magnification, might notice how effective Halley's efforts have been to make his paintings appear as computational artefacts. It is this analogy between the two-dimensional images of chip diagrams and the painted canvas that I will use to explain how some painting seems to point to possibilities outside the universalisations of Turing machines and the totalisations of Baudrillard's simulacra.

Chains and Alphabets

I will start with alphabets. As McLuhan and others have pointed out, the invention of moveable type made Guttenberg's press one of the first Western machines of mass production.[57] Machines of mass production require a fixed 'alphabet', eg, the 26 letters plus a few punctuation marks needed to print books in the English language. Turing's machine is no different. His theoretical formulation employs a pre-defined fixed alphabet of symbols (cf, his original paper[58] or any textbook introduction to the subject[59]). Interestingly, Turing (parenthetically) brings up a means of disputing the adequacy of a restricted symbol set in the discussion section of his original paper:

I shall suppose that the number of symbols which may be

FROM ABOVE: Lydia Dona, Occupants Within The Gaze On The Nerves Of Urban Tissues, *1995, acrylic, oil, and sign paint on canvas, 213.4 x 162.6cm*

printed is finite. If we were to allow an infinity of symbols, then there would be symbols differing to an arbitrarily small extent. The effect of this restriction of the number of symbols is not very serious. It is always possible to use sequences of symbols in the place of single symbols. Thus an Arabic numeral such as 17 or 999999999999999 is normally treated as a single symbol. Similarly, in any European language words are treated as single symbols, although Chinese attempts to have an innumerable infinity of symbols.[60]

Yet, how easy is it to think of written Chinese without at least glancing attention to the arts of calligraphy? Calligraphers produce more than an innumerable infinity of symbols; calligraphers produce an infinity of symbols each differing from the others 'to an arbitrarily small extent'. Yes, if we maintain a schematic reduction of Chinese – or hand written European prose for that matter – we can forget the infinite variations and productions of script. But, such a reduction is an idealisation which marginalises the role of gesture and the production of signs in writing, drawing and painting.

I am reminded of an off-hand remark once made by Henri Matisse in which he proposed that truly important artists introduce a great number of new signs into the arts.[61] As an example, Matisse explained how many artists learn how to paint the foliage on trees by repeatedly brushing '33' on the area of the canvas that is suppose to correspond to the leaves of the plant while other, more interesting artists, invent new ways of approaching the same problem of abstraction. One must employ a certain kind of fuzzy vision to ignore the inventions Matisse describes: the infinitely multiplying and complicated 'alphabets' of, for example, the 'New York Artists' mentioned by Danto in his remarks on 'painting-as-writing'. It is exactly the ever-expanding alphabets that Turing takes as insignificant and forgettable in the construction of his machines that Deleuze and Guattari take as central to the construction of theirs:

No chain is homogeneous; all of them resemble, rather, a succession of characters from different alphabets in which an ideogram, a pictogram, a tiny image of an elephant passing by, or a rising sun may suddenly make its appearance. In a chain that mixes together phonemes, morphemes, etc without combining them, papa's moustache, mama's upraised arm, a ribbon, a little girl, a cup, a shoe suddenly turn up.[62]

What remains unclear about Matisse's comment and Deleuze and Guattari's subscription to heterogeneous, multiplying alphabets and sign systems is who, or what, is allowed to introduce a new sign? As the Guerrilla Girls and Linda Nochlin's famous essay, 'Why Have There Been No Great Women Artists?'[63], make clear, it is often not the women who are allowed to transform or produce signs for strategic spaces of interaction, like the galleries and museums of painting. This general problematic, of what has been called 'feminist epistemology'[64],

is left unresolved by a discussion which focuses exclusively on gesture and the formal production of signs. But by tying such a discussion to the possibilities of producing a different (perhaps non-computational) machinery, the ethical issues at stake can be explored. Crucial to any ethical investigation of machinery is a determination of who has been automated 'out of the loop'? Whose position or role has been replaced by the machine, or repressed by the implemented machinery?

Within the critical discourse of Baudrillardian 'simulationist' art a recurrent thematic of the 'death of the artist' or a 'death of the author' (in Foucault's[65] sense or Barthes'[66] sense) was detectable (cf, several of the essays in the *Endgame* catalogue[67]). However, if the artist is 'dead', ie, 'automated out of the loop', then do the names of any artists still have to be mentioned? Obviously we have not entered upon a point in art history, much less art criticism, in which names are optional. Consequently, the question becomes who needs to be cited? For example, when one notes the mechanical diagrams that can often be seen in Lydia Dona's paintings, does one need to note that they are Duchamp-like in some sense? Or, can one simply say that Dona has produced a novel set of mechanical marks? As far as I can tell, neither Baudrillard's simulacra, nor even the adoption of the infinite, heterogeneous 'chains' or alphabets of Deleuze and Guattari allow us to escape the political questions raised by a regime of the *auteur*[68] and the politics of the signature.[69]

Grids and Smooth Space

If a fixed, predetermined alphabet is Turing's first requirement for the construction of his machine, then a bureaucratic attention to the grid is the second requirement:

Computing is normally done by writing certain symbols on paper. We may suppose this paper is divided into squares like a child's arithmetic book . . . I assume then that the computation is carried out on one-dimensional paper, ie, on a tape divided into squares.[70]

It can be shown, from a mathematical perspective, that Turing machines with one-dimensional tapes are just as powerful as machines with two-dimensional tapes. However, within the construct of a computational system, one cannot escape the 'squares', the grid. If a sign slides out of the grid or exceeds its allotted area of one 'square' (not two or more), a computational apparatus of Turing's design simply scans each square individually and assigns to each square a 'value' of one of the symbols of the predefined alphabet it has been built around. In a sense, the machines are designed to deny them the possible cognitive state of the Kantian sublime, the moment of indecision when a phenomenon cannot be coerced into a known schema. Turing's 'squares' are, in Deleuze and Guattari's vocabulary, a strictly 'striated space' (as opposed to a 'smooth space').[71] In contrast, Deleuze and Guattari assume that their machines are interruptions in 'smooth', borderless, flowing space.

Many painters have understood the radical possibilities born of a violation of the grid. I must admit though, it has only been by feeling these transgressions through a Deleuzean prosthetic that I have been able to grasp the investments in the grid made implicitly by software developers. These grids are not simply the pixelated patterns one can see on one's computer screen; they are the grids which can be found at every level of existing computer architecture because of Turing's initial commitment to the grid in his definition of the Turing machine. To see, for example, painter Valerie Jaudon's invented 'alphabets' imposed over and traversing a background grid (as in, for example, her painting *Accomplice*, 1991), is to imagine an 'impossible' computer machine design.

The software engineer will object at this point. If we were able to take the flowing paint that breaks an underlying grid (in the manner that Valerie Jaudon's or Marien Schouten's foregrounded marks break a 'background' grid) and try to 'reverse engineer' it (ie, to search for both the mechanical 'interpreter' or 'compiler' and the idiomatic sequence of machine instructions which would allow the paint to be seen as a computer program) our efforts would not produce a machine that 'works' in the opinion of the software engineer.[72] Again though, I would contest that this objection is incomplete with respect to the debates of feminist epistemology and situated knowledge.[73] Specifically, the question begged is this one: For whom would such a machine not work?

A machine, as sociologist of science Bruno Latour points out, is a kind of *machination*.[74] Obviously as a machination, a painting does work for someone, even a whole group of people: the painting is a machination which holds painter, dealer, gallery owner, museum director, art audience, canvas and pigments together. Thus, questioning the maintenance of the grid can lead to an exploration of the idea that machines based on the grid, like the computer, 'work' for some people and against others. In a similar manner painting-machines can work for some and against others.

Details and Abstraction

My third, consideration concerns 'details'. Which 'details' can be abstracted away from a text, painting, or machine? For example, Turing's machines are based upon a certain type of 'forgetting' in order to allow him (or, now, contemporary computer scientists) to build them as 'discrete state machines':

> Strictly speaking there are no such [discrete state] machines. Everything really moves continuously. But there are many kinds of machines which can profitably be thought of as being discrete state machines. For instance, in considering the switch for a lighting system it is a convenient fiction that each switch must be definitely on or definitely off. There must be intermediate positions, but for most purposes we can forget about them.[75]

Note that Turing's rationale is an economical, teleological construction that depends upon what is 'profitable', 'convenient', and what 'for most purposes we can forget about'. Essentially, Turing asks us to perform a sort of goal-based 'abstraction', a metonymic displacement created by selecting a discrete set of states from a continuously moving world. Turing's moving world is probably a borrowed image from his physicist-colleagues. It is nevertheless striking that his description of 'everything' here resembles the constant flux, flows, and chains of Deleuze and Guattari. Also, like Deleuze and Guattari, Turing sees the genesis of a machine in the interruption of this constant motion. However, Deleuze and Guattari's interruptions or 'abstractions', seem quite different from Turing's purposeful isolations:

> By contrast in Deleuze one finds an abstraction concerned not with extracting 'information' from things (as though the material world were so much clumsy hardware), but rather with finding within things the delicate, complicated 'abstract' virtualities of other things. Such abstraction doesn't entail independence or transferability from material support and doesn't operate according to a logic of simulation. Rather, inherent in materials, it supposes the subsistence of connections which exceed the messages of a medium, and ourselves as senders and receivers of them.[76]

Abstract painter Lydia Dona expands upon John Rajchman's insight with respect to her own work:

> Demetrio Paparoni: So a painting is not a simulation?
> Lydia Dona: No, a painting is not a simulation, because in simulation there is only one aspect, a facade.[77] Nevertheless a painting contains certain traits of simulation, since it addresses the question of artificiality (while at the same time going beyond artificiality). I'm interested in the fracture or friction of different models that break down in a techno-urban environment, so for me the question of reality is fluidity.[78]

To construct a Turing machine we must isolate out certain features of a continuous flow. This mechanical logic requires one to see certain details as irrelevant. In contrast, Deleuze and Guattari ask us to see a machine as a set of interruptions and as a set of connections or links.[79] Thus, any detail might serve as a connection to something outside of the machine-painting.

> The machinic painters stressed the following: that they did not paint machines as substitutes for still lifes or nudes; the machine is not a represented object anymore than the drawing of it is a representation. The aim is to introduce an element of a machine, so that it combines with something else on the full body of the canvas, be it with the painting itself, with the result that it is precisely the ensemble of the painting that functions as a desiring-machine. The induced machine is always other than the one that appears to be represented.[80]

Yet, 'what appears to be represented' in a painting, a machine, or a painting-machine is not a trivial issue. Whose details are intensified (and so abstracted in the Deleuzean sense) or forgotten (and so abstracted in a Platonic sense)?

Signs, Grids and Details

This essay, which isolates formal, technical details of Turing machines and Deleuze and Guattari's machines in order to argue for a type of 'autonomous' (ie, 'autonomous' from techno-science) position for painting is avant-gardist[81] in character because of its focus on a conjunction of formal details and autonomy. I have isolated three distinctions between Turing machines and 'desiring machines' and have used painting to illustrate these distinctions: (1) Signs: the prohibition or acceptance of a heterogeneous, expanding 'alphabet' of signs or marks; (2) Grids: the transgression or adherence to the boundaries of the grid; (3) Details: the attention to different kinds of details and the forgetting, intensification or 'abstraction' of others.

It is the third point, 'details', which gives this essay its focus and philosophical underpinnings. Details read through Deleuze and Guattari's theory of machines push one to examine how small variations and minutia connect an artefact, like a painting, to a larger 'outside' world. Deleuze and Guattari encourage us to see an infinity of details connecting a desiring machine to others: 'What defines desiring-machines is precisely their capacity for an unlimited number of connections, in every sense and in all directions.'[82]

It is this insight that can inspire one to stand up close to a painting and see a larger significance in the brushstrokes and small variations in pigment. However, it is not just the details, but even more importantly, it is the 'unlimited number of connections' that these details can engender that separates this kind of avant-gardist (or, in Guattari's sense 'ethico-aesthetic') 'reading' from a technoscientific reading. One can tell a convincing narrative about the convergence of Deleuze and Guattari's machines, Turing's work in automata theory (ie, 'Turing machines') and artificial intelligence, and the emergence and development of contemporary scientific and technical work in chaos theory, complexity and artificial intelligence. For example, Manuel De Landa narrates a convergence of these issues in his book *War in the Age of Intelligence Machines*[83] by embedding them all in a genealogy of weapons and sophisticated war machines. Nevertheless, I think it is important to keep in mind that the technoscientific elements of this constellation of subjects (eg, theories of chaos, complexity and work in artificial intelligence) are aimed at containing chaos, producing intelligent machines of automation to isolate or eliminate functions which are now performed by humans, and to find limits and boundaries of complexity; they are strategies of containment, isolation and control.

In strong contrast to this is a reading of Deleuze and Guattari's perspective which emphasises an infinity of connections rather than the enumeration of finite limits or possible boundaries. Although the theoretics of Deleuze and Guattari can give one a new appreciation for details, a more sociological approach[84] to artistic reception may be required to answer the types of questions that I found myself repeating but not addressing as completely as I would like to: for whom is a detail not important? Who is allowed to produce new signs? Whose space can be divided by whom and in what manner?

Notes

1 'Bakhtin described a transference or subjectivisation operating between the author and the contemplator of a work of art – the "spectator" in Marcel Duchamp's sense. According to Bakhtin, in this movement the "consumer" in some way becomes co-creator', Félix Guattari, *Chaosmosis: An Ethico-Aesthetic Paradigm*, Paul Bains and Julian Pefanis (trans), Indiana University Press, Bloomington, 1995, p14.

2 See, for example, Jean Baudrillard, *Selected Writings,* Mark Poster (ed), Stanford University Press, Stanford, 1988, pp166-84.

3 Hal Foster, 'Signs Taken for Wonders', *Art in America,* June 1986, p88.

4 See, for example, the art and artists discussed in the *Journal of Philosophy and the Visual Arts, Abstraction,* No 5, Academy Editions, London, 1995. These include Jackson Pollock, Francis Bacon, Marcel Duchamp, Gerhard Richter, Lydia Dona, David Reed, Jessica Stockholder, Stephen Ellis, Fabian Marcaccio, Polly Apfelbaum, and others.

5 *op cit* Guattari, pp100-101.

6 *ibid*, p10.

7 Brian Massumi, 'The Autonomy of Affect', *Cultural Critique (The Politics of Systems and Environments, Part II)* Number 31, Fall 1995, p93.

8 Manuel De Landa, *War in the Age of Intelligent Machines,* Zone Books, New York, 1991, pp234-37.

9 Gilles Deleuze, *Logic of Sense,* Mark Lester (trans) Constantin V Boundas (ed), Columbia University Press, New York, 1990, Chapter 15.

10 Alan M Turing 'On Computable Numbers, with an Application to the *Entscheidungsproblem, Proceedings, London Mathematical Society,* 2, No 42,1936, pp230-65.

11 Alan Turing 'Computing Machinery and Intelligence,' *Mind,* Volume LIX, No 236, 1950.

12 Jean-François Lyotard, *The Differend: Phrases in Dispute,* University of Minnesota Press, Minneapolis, 1988.

13 *op cit,* Turing, 'On Computable Numbers . . . , pp230-65; an English translation of Kurt Gödel's original paper can be found in Martin Davis (ed), *The Undecidable,* Raven Press, New York, 1965. For clear, yet less mathematical descriptions of these proofs, see Andrew Hodges' *Alan Turing: The Enigma,* Simon and Schuster, New York, 1983; see also Douglas Hofstadter, Gödel, Escher, *Bach: An Eternal Golden Braid,* Vintage Books, New York, 1979.

Peter Halley, Stairway to Heaven, *1992, Day-Glo acrylic, acrylic, Roll-a-tex on canvas, 242.6 x 218.4cm (photo, Steven Sloman)*

14 The 'mathematical sublime' is theorised by Immanuel Kant in his *Critique of Judgement*, Hafner Press, New York, 1951, pp86-96.

15 Jean-François Lyotard, *Lessons on the Analytic of the Sublime,* Elizabeth Rottenberg (trans), Stanford University Press, Stanford, 1994.

16 I think it is at least passingly interesting to note, as Lyotard does in the passage below, that the sublime forms a link between thinkers like Kant and the very different lineage of thinkers that Deleuze draws from to establish a theory of the subject which is not based on lack (eg, Masoch, Spinoza, Nietzsche, and others). 'Le sentiment sublime, qui est aussi le sentiment du sublime, est selon Kant une affection forte et équivoque: il comporte à la fois plaisir et peine. Mieux: le plaisir y procède de la peine. Dans la tradition de la philosophie du sujet qui vient d'Augustin et de Descartes et que Kant ne remet pas en cause radicalement, cette contradiction que d'autres appelleraient névrose ou masochisme, se développe comme un conflit entre les facultés d'un sujet, la faculté de concevoir quelque chose et la faculté de 'présenter' quelque chose'. Jean-François Lyotard, *Le Postmoderne expliqué aux enfants*, Galilée, Paris, 1988, pp24-25.

17 'All the time and space of [the worker's] world become foreign to him with the accumulation of his alienated products. The spectacle is the map of this new world, a map which exactly covers its territory.' Guy Debord, *Society of the Spectacle*, MIT Press, Cambridge, Mass, 1995.

18 Jean Baudrillard, *Selected Writings*, Mark Poster (ed), Stanford University Press, Stanford, 1988, p166.

19 *ibid*, p167.

20 The 'Pictures' show included artists such as Troy Brauntuch, Jack Goldstein, Sherrie Levine, Robert Longo and Philip Smith.

21 For example, Barbara Kruger, Robert Longo, Richard Prince, Jack Goldstein and Sherrie Levine showed at the Metro Pictures Gallery in the late 70s and early 80s.

22 Peter Halley, Jeff Koons, Ashley Bickerton and Meyer Vaisman all 'escaped' from the East Village to the SoHo Sonnabend Gallery in 1986; others did the same soon thereafter.

23 Christina Lodder, *Russian Constructivism*, Yale University Press, New Haven, 1983; Benjamin HD Buchloh, 'From Faktura to Factography', *October* 30, Fall 1984.

24 'What I am saying is that media as extensions of our senses institute new ratios, not only among our private senses, but among themselves, when they interact among themselves. Radio changed the form of the news story as much as it altered the film image in the talkies. TV caused drastic changes in radio programming, and in the form of the thing or documentary novel. It is the poets and painters who react instantly to a new medium like radio or TV.' from Marshall McLuhan *Understanding Media: the Extensions of Man*, McGraw-Hill, New York, 1964.

25 Clement Greenberg, *Works: Clement Greenberg: the Collected Essays and Criticism*, University of Chicago Press, Chicago, 1986-1993.

26 Peter Halley, Sherrie Levine, Philip Taaffe, Ross Bleckner, Jeff Koons, Haim Steinbach, General Idea, Joel Otterson, Jon Kessler, Richard Baim, Gretchen Bender, and Perry Hoberman were the artists shown at the Boston ICA *Endgame* show. ICA Boston, *Endgame: Reference and Simulation in Recent Painting and Sculpture*, MIT Press, Cambridge, Mass, 1986.

27 'So far I have argued that many of the significant redefinitions of the (post)modern work of art are in fact fetishistic responses to contradictions between different economies of the object; that many of these contradictions are in turn cast up by the dialectic of modernism and mass culture; and that it is these contradictions – such as the one between functional product and dysfunctional art work – that the readymade has served to articulate'. Hal Foster, 'The Future of an Illusion, or The Contemporary Artist as Cargo Cultist', in the catalogue *Endgame, op cit* note 26, p100.

28 *op cit*, Foster, 'Signs Taken for Wonders'.

29 Gilles Deleuze, 'Plato and the Simulacrum', Rosalind Krauss (trans) *October* 27, Winter 1983.

30 *op cit* Foster, 'Signs Taken for Wonders'.

31 John Rajchman, 'Another View of Abstraction', *Journal of Philosophy and the Visual Arts, Abstraction*, No 5, Academy Editions, London 1995, pp16-24.

32 *ibid*, p17.

33 Gilles Deleuze, 'Plato and the Simulacrum', Rosalind Krauss (trans), *October* 27, Winter 1983.

34 Gilles Deleuze, *Difference and Repetition*, Columbia University Press, New York, 1994.

35 *op cit*, Deleuze, *Logic of Sense*.

36 *op cit*, Deleuze, *Difference and Repetition*, p 63.

37 *op cit*, Deleuze, 'Plato and the Simulacrum', p47.

38 Vladímir Propp, *Morphology of the Folktale,* Second Edition Louis A Wagner (trans), University of Texas Press, Austin, 1968.

39 Claude Lévi-Strauss, *Structural Anthropology*, C Jacobson and BG Schoepf (trans), Doubleday, Garden City, New York, 1967.

40 Algirdas Julien Greimas, *On Meaning: Selected Writings in Semiotic Theory*, Paul J Perron and Frank H Collins (trans), University of Minnesota Press, Minneapolis, 1987.

41 'We can thus better define the whole of the Platonic motive – it is a matter of choosing claimants, of distinguishing the good from the false copies, or even more, the always well-founded copies from the simulacra, ever corrupted by the dissemblance. It is a question of insuring the triumph of the copies over the simulacra, of repressing the simulacra, of keeping them chained in the depths, of preventing them from rising to the surface and 'insinuating' themselves everywhere', *op cit*, Deleuze, 'Plato and the Simulacrum', p48.

42 *op cit*, Deleuze 'Plato and the Simulacrum', pp51-52; and Deleuze, *Difference and Repetition*, p67.

43 *op cit*, Gilles Deleuze 'Plato and the Simulacrum', p53.

44 Gilles Deleuze and Félix Guattari, *Anti-Oedipus: Capitalism and Schizophrenia*, Viking Press, New York, 1977.

45 *See Journal of Philosophy and the Visual Arts, Abstraction*.

46 *op cit*, Deleuze and Guattari, *Anti-Oedipus: Capitalism and Schizophrenia*, p41.

47 *ibid*, pp36-41.

48 *ibid*, p36.

49 *op cit*, Rajchman.

50 *ibid*, p22.

51 op cit, Alan Turing 'Computing Machinery and Intelligence'.

52 *ibid.*

53 Arthur Danto, 'Painting and Writing', *New York Painters* (catalogue), Sammlung Goetz, München, p12.

54 From 'Peter Halley makes a move . . .', Jeff Rian, *Flash Art International* Vol XXXIII, no184, October 1995, p91.

55 *ibid*, p92.

56 *op cit*, Deleuze and Guattari, *Anti-Oedipus* p273.

57 Marshall McLuhan, *The Guttenberg Gallaxy: The Making of Typographical Man,* University of Toronto Press, Toronto, 1962.

58 *op cit*, Turing, 'On Computable Numbers', pp230-265.

59 Harry Lewis and Christos Papadimitrious, *Elements of the Theory of Computation*, Prentice-Hall, Englewood Cliffs,1981, p168.

60 *op cit*, Turing, 'On Computable Numbers', pp249-50.

61 'L'importance d'un artiste se mesure à la quantité de nouveaux signes qu'il aura introduits dans le language plastique', from 'Propos sur le dessin de l'arbre rapportés par Louis Aragon,' in *Henri Matisse: Ecrits et propos sur l'art,* Herman, Paris, 1972, p172.

62 *op cit*, Deleuze and Guattari, *Anti-Oedipus*, p39.

63 Nochlin's essay 'Why Have There Been No Great Women Artists?' can be found in her book Linda Nochlin, *Women, Art, and Power: and Other Essays*, Harper & Row, New York, 1988.

64 Sandra G Harding, *Whose Science? Whose Knowledge? Thinking From Women's Lives*, Cornell University Press, Ithaca, 1991.

65 Michel Foucault, 'What is an author?', *Language, Counter-Memory, Practice: Selected Essays and Interviews*, Donald F Bouchard (ed), Donald F Bouchard and Sherry Sim (trans), Cornell University Press, Ithaca, 1977.

66 Roland Barthes, 'The Death of the Author', *Image, music, text*, Stephen Heath (trans), Fontana, London, 1977.

67 *op cit*, *Endgame*.

68 Stephen Heath, Comment on 'The idea of authorship', *Screen* 14, p3.

69 Jacques Derrida *Limited Inc*, Johns Hopkins University Press, Baltimore, 1977.

70 *op cit*,Turing, 'On Computable Numbers', p249.

71 Gilles Deleuze and Félix Guattari, *A Thousand Plateaus: Capitalism and Schizophrenia*, University of Minnesota Press, Minneapolis, 1987, pp492-99.

72 'It is futile to examine the usefulness or uselessness, the possibility or impossibility of these desiring-machines. Their impossibility and their uselessness become visible only in the autonomous artistic presentation, and there very rarely. Don't you see that they are possible because they are; they are there in every way, and we function with them. They are eminently useful, since they constitute the two directions of the relationship between the machine and man, the *communication* of the two. At the very moment you say, "this machine is impossible", you fail to see that you are making it possible by being yourself one of its parts, the very part that you seemed to be missing in order for it to be already working, the dancer-danger. You argue about the possibility or the usefulness, but you are already inside the machine, you are a part of it, you have put a finger inside, or an eye, your anus, or your liver (the modern version of "You are embarked . . . ")' *Semiotext(e)*, D&G, p129.

73 *op cit*, Harding.

74 The simplest means of transforming the juxtaposed set of allies into a whole that acts as one is to tie the assembled forces *to one another*, that is, to build a machine. A machine, as its name implies, is first of all, a machination, a stratagem, a kind of cunning, where borrowed forces keep one another in check so that none can fly apart from the group. Bruno Latour, 1987, *Science in Action: How to Follow Scientists and Engineers Through Society*, Harvard University Press, Cambridge, Mass, pp128-29.

75 *op cit*, Turing, as cited in Andrew Hodges, *Alan Turing*, p419.

76 *op cit*, Rajchman, p22.

77 Lydia Dona's reference to 'simulation' in this quote appears, to me, to be a reference to either computational simulations and/or Baudrillard's simulacra but not to Deleuze's simulacra.

78 Demetrio Paparoni, 'Lydia Dona: a conversation with Demetrio Paparoni', *Tema Celeste Art Magazine, Special Issue: New Forms of Abstraction* (First Part), Autumn 1991, pp90-91.

79 Deleuze and Guattari's 'interruptions' and 'connections' are analogous to Marshall McLuhan's media 'amputations' and 'extensions'.

80 Deleuze and Guatarri, 'Balance Sheet – Program for Desiring-Machines', *Semiotext(e)* Volume II, no 3, 1977, p121.

81 Peter Bürger, *Theory of the Avant-Garde*, Michael Shaw (trans), University of Minnesota Press, Minneapolis, 1984.

82 *op cit*, Deleuze and Guatari, 'Balance Sheet – Program for Desiring-Machines', p121.

83 *op cit*, De Landa.

84 For instance, sociologist Pierre Bourdieu and artist Hans Haacke, in their respective work, have created sociological approaches to answering questions like these about art. An interesting introduction to their independent contributions can be found in their joint conversation/book, Pierre Bourdieu and Hans Haacke, *Free Exchange*, Stanford University Press, Stanford, CA, 1995.

Philip Taaffe, Mosaic, *1991, mixed media on linen, 284.8 x 189.2cm*